G. O'Reilly Allen

Chip On My Shoulder

By

G.I. "Mickey" O'Reilly Allen

Copyright © Genevieve Allen – December 2003

For information on this book email:

Mimi: tmitchell3@juno.com

**Instant Publisher.com
P. O. Box 985
Collierville, TN 38027**

Dedicated to all the nurses of WWII

who loved all the great guys just as much as I did

Acknowledgements

I would like to thank my granddaughter's husband, Todd Cavaleri, for printing a collection of stories I had written and for distributing them to other grandchildren. They encouraged me to write more stories, which are now part of this book.

To my first born, Mary Mitchell, who loved the stories so much that she wanted to publish this work when it was originally only six chapters long. She gets all the credit for publishing this.

To my dear niece and editor, Catherine O'Reilly, who encouraged me to start this book ten years ago. Her unending chant of 'just one more line' moved me to add phrases, sentences and paragraphs that led to the completion of this work.

Foreword

How can a senior citizen, who calls all her children and grandchildren by the wrong name and has to leave memos to herself all over the house, write a story about events that happened to her over 60 years ago? Simple--most of these stories have been told so many times, to so many people, that they have become rote.

My oldest daughter Mary told me that when all my kids were young, they knew if they asked me a question about the Army at bedtime it would put off prayers and going to bed for at least half an hour. They learned at an early age how to turn my mouth on.

Another contributing factor was that my father, under the illusion that I was the bravest, most brilliant and heroic nurse in the Army Nurse Corps, kept every letter I wrote home and placed them into two albums. They numbered over 250.

I got into the habit of writing home every two or three days, primarily so Mom and Pop would know that I was O.K. I soon realized, however, that writing home actually brought me home, even if only for a few minutes. I could almost feel their presence as I wrote the letters. I tried to omit the morbid events and never wrote on Sunday, the day I was usually depressed.

Remarkably now, opening to any page in the albums transports me back in time and space to North Africa or Italy. Not only do I remember the events in detail, but I can almost smell the canvas tent and feel the heat or coldness of the day in the letter I am reading.

I was embarrassed when I returned home and my father presented me with the two albums. I put them in the bottom of the bookcase and tried to forget about them. I knew I was not, and could never hope to be, all that Pop thought I was. I was just one of many devoted nurses during WWII. If we hadn't cared about the guys, we never would have been able to endure.

Thanks to the fact that my father saved these albums, I can recall vivid memories where I normally would have had only slight recollections. Perhaps others may have more interesting or funnier tales to tell, but I would like to share my story on behalf of all the veteran nurses of World War II.

Thanks for the memories, Pop!

CHAPTER I

I love to tell people that I was born in Brooklyn and grew up in Africa. It amazes people when I tell them that, but it is absolutely true, even though I was 22 years old when I landed on African soil.

I was born in Brooklyn, NY, in 1919, the baby of the family and the only girl, with four older brothers.

I attended Catholic school for 12 years, and in senior year of high school I found myself seriously considering the idea of becoming a nun. All of my life I had wanted to be a nurse, but this convent idea was also taking up a lot of my thoughts and time. I thought how wonderful it would be to combine the two. Good thinking--a nursing nun. Be all that you can be. Strive for all your dreams, just like all the books say.

I decided to discuss my vocation with Sister Mary Louise, a Dominican nun who was also my favorite teacher. She was very surprised to hear about this new concept, since up to that point I had only spoken to her about being a nurse. All my classmates and other teachers knew about my nursing ambitions as well, and smiled at my new idea--they believed that adding a religious vocation to that aim was pushing my credibility.

Sister Mary Louise explained that to be accepted into the convent as a novice, my superiors would have to be certain that my religious vocation was stronger than my nursing one. She said I might even be trained as a teacher, rather than a nurse, to test the validity of my calling.

I honestly believed that I could not go through with that arrangement and that it would be smarter and easier for me to get my R.N. and then enter the convent. I decided I would ask God to wait three years for me and told Sister Mary Louise that I would pray about it. It was the first of many conversations we would have. I was very fortunate to have her in my life, and was very happy when she later became my mentor.

So in September, 1939, I entered nurses' training at Norwegian Lutheran Hospital in Brooklyn, NY (Lutheran to guarantee that the Catholic Church wouldn't get me before the R.N. deal came through.)

Everyone, except President Bush, knows that Pearl Harbor was bombed on December 7, 1941, drawing the U.S. into the war. I had two brothers in the Navy at the time, and knew I had to go. I wanted the Army. Kate Smith was singing "God Bless America" and I had to be in the action. So I prayed again and asked God if He would wait for me until it was over, knowing that the length of the duration would be entirely up to Him.

In my senior year of training, the Army came up with an idea called "Student Reserve." This meant signing up in senior year before graduation and State Boards. It would give the Army plenty of time to investigate candidates. They wanted people who were easily molded, could be blindly led, mindless, and fit for a commission.

I immediately signed up, graduated, and when the State Board Examiners passed me (the awesome power of prayer), I got a date from the Government of the United States to appear for my physical examination.

I had been working the night shift from 7 p.m. to 7 a.m. (those were the good old days) and when I got off duty I took a subway from Brooklyn to Whitehall Street, New York City, where the physical was to be held. I think it was the second time I had ever made the journey to New

York by myself. When the doctor on duty, a Major, saw my application form, he laughed long and loud.

He asked me if my name was really Genevieve Inez O'Reilly. I told him yes, it was (and though I was named after my aunt and thought it was a little weird, especially since she never named one of her three daughters Inez, I never thought it was all that funny.) Well, he told me, all of my Army papers from that point on were going to read Lieutenant G.I. O'Reilly, and if I didn't think it was funny then, I certainly would when I got to understand Army lingo. He proved correct, because many enlisted men in my outfit called me G.I.

The very first thing the eminent doctor did was to take my blood pressure. He pulled the stethoscope out of his ears and told me no--it would never do--that my blood pressure was way too low. I explained that I had been up for 18 hours, 12 of which were spent running a surgical floor, and that I was just a little pooped. He finally agreed it would be O.K., but said I would have to sign a waiver releasing the U.S. Government of any responsibility for my low blood pressure. I signed the waiver.

Next he tested my hearing. Because he knew that I had spent three years at Norwegian Hospital, he whispered a Norwegian phrase in my ear, which translated to "I love you" (he said later the only reason he knew the term was because he had heard it in a song somewhere before. Right...) I responded with the phrase that meant, "Oh, do you love me really." We both laughed, and so I passed my hearing test.

Not to digress, but I should never really mess around with speaking Norwegian. We used to work at the hospital from 7 a.m. to 7 p.m., with three hours off in between. Many of the nurses were Norwegian and when they were going on break they would say, in their native tongue, "I think I shall go home and lay myself down to sleep," a phrase I picked up on.

As students, if we returned to the residence after 9:00 p.m., we would have to report to the Emergency Room and call the night watchman, who was a very sweet old Norwegian man. He would then escort us across the street and let us in. One night I came in late and called him as required. To show off how smart I was, I repeated the Norwegian phrase I had heard so many times before. Unfortunately, I mistakenly used the word 'you' instead of 'me' which translated to "I shall go home and lay you." The poor old guy almost had a coronary from laughing, and the next day word was all over the hospital that "Mickey had propositioned the night watchman."

I suppose this is a good time to explain the reason why everyone calls an old lady like myself Mickey. There were 13 of us in the class, some of whom were named Williamson, Nordlund, Jenson, Johnson, Hansome, Jorgenson and me, O'Reilly. Well, it all began when everyone in school started calling me "the Mick." By graduation it had become Mickey to everyone in the hospital. When I went to Ft. Monmouth, a girl I had gone to school with was also there and she introduced me as Mickey. I carried that name through the Army and was introduced to my future husband that way. When we got home from the war, he introduced me to friends and family as Mick, and that still stands, even though it sounds foolish when you look at this wrinkled face. It got to the point where I couldn't change it, though, and today 24 grandchildren and nine great grandchildren call me Grandma Mick.

To go back in time to the Army physical: The Major, after the hearing test, looked at my feet and told me--no way. No way. He told me I had bilateral, 3rd degree pes plantes, which in layman's terms meant that both feet were as flat as they could possibly be. (Plaster casts of them were made while I was in training and the doctor kept them because he said they looked like beautiful Indian moccasins. In truth, you couldn't slip a piece of paper between either foot and the floor.)

The good Major told me no--my feet were too flat. I asked him what the problem was--that I was going to be nursing, not marching. He asked me what I would do if a bomb fell. To prove how fast I could really move I raced across the floor, but accidentally crashed into a chair, which made considerable noise. Seconds later, a Captain and Sergeant came running into the room to see what the hell was going on, and chuckled when they realized what had happened. When they left and the Major and I were alone again in the examining room, we discussed the foot problem. Once again we agreed that I should sign a waiver to rid the U.S. Government of any responsibility as to my flat feet. Waiver #2.

The Major remarked that it had been a very interesting morning. He told me that he was the officer in charge, and hardly ever did physical exams. He handed me a specimen bottle and said, "I'm sure you are going to make it into the Army. Just get me a urine sample. Put it on the shelf in the other room on top of this slip." He wrote "G.I. O'Reilly" on the lab form, patted me on the shoulder and sent me on my way.

I went into the john and got the specimen. It occurred to me that although I felt good and was in fair shape, I had consumed many, many cups of coffee. I also remembered that 15 years before, I had had a slight urinary infection. What the hell, I figured--best not take a chance on anything being wrong with this urine. So I came out, went to the shelf where there were about ten other samples, and swapped mine with someone else's--I knew not whom. I knew if they called me on this, I could always come back and give them a sample of my own. I wasn't about to risk waiver #3, because 3 and you're out.

To a person of normal intelligence this whole experience would have been a clear indication of 'things to come' in my new life as an Army Nurse. Two waivers and someone else's pee.

I told Miss Jones, the nursing supervisor at Norwegian, that I had taken my Army physical. Knowing of my flat feet she said, "Mickey, they will take you when Hitler marches down Fourth Avenue."

On February 16 I went into her office, took her by the hand and led her over to the window. With great pleasure I said, "Look, Miss Jones. Here comes Hitler." Miss Jones looked at me lovingly and said, "Look out, Army. Here comes Mickey."

I reported to Ft. Monmouth and was sworn into the Army as a 2nd Lieutenant on February 18, 1943.

CHAPTER II

I was at Ft. Monmouth for about two weeks, just getting used to Army life, when a new chief nurse was assigned to the station hospital. She had just returned from serving two years in the Fiji Islands, and decided to do away with the list of 'alerted' nurses that had previously been posted. From her experience she felt that overseas duty should be on a volunteer basis, not just assigned by the brass. She took down the old list and put up a paper asking for volunteers. I got to the sign-up sheet and was amazed to see the number of names on the list. Some of the names surprised me because I knew those nurses were on night duty and had to get out of bed to sign up. I said a quick prayer and added my name to the list.

I became so immersed in all the new Army techniques and procedures that I forgot all about it.

About two weeks later I went to the mess hall for supper. I got my food, sat at a table and started to eat when I noticed that everyone seemed to be 'hyped up.'

"What's up?" I asked.

"The new list is up," someone replied, as another nurse dashed from the table. Big deal, I thought to myself, and kept on eating.

"Isn't your name O'Reilly?" someone asked.

"Yes," I replied.

"Well, your name is on the list."

"Big deal" I said out loud.

"Well, you're either a real cool cat or a damned good actress," she said as I continued to eat.

"Look," I said, "I have been here for three weeks and have been expecting to get stuck on night duty since I got here. All new hands always get stuck on nights and I can't get all excited about a night duty list."

"Night Duty list, you jerk!" she screamed. "This list is for overseas duty!"

I couldn't swallow the food in my mouth. I guess I turned green, because everyone laughed and someone said, "Not so cool."

I had the strangest feeling as I walked over slowly to the bulletin board. I wasn't happy or sad--just frightened. My chest felt tight and my knees felt like they were going to buckle. I felt frightened for the first time in my life. There was the neatly typed notice--'Alerted For Overseas Duty'--and in the middle of the list, 'O'Reilly,' spelled correctly and legibly for all to see.

CHAPTER III

Ordinary days changed from the moment I was put on 'alert' to go overseas. This meant that I could not leave the post. Finally I was given an eight-hour pass to go to New York and get what personal items I would need to take with me.

I took off for Brooklyn. I had five hours to say goodbye to my family. When I reached home, my mother, sister-in-law Kay (more a sister than in-law), nephew Jackie and youngest brother Jack (who was on leave from the Navy) were there. I decided not to tell anyone that this was going to be my last time home. I thought it would be easier that way. I just said I was home to pick up some belongings.

We had lunch and I was very proud of how well I kept myself under control. I wondered how long it would be before I would see them again.

I couldn't believe the feelings of sadness that enveloped me as I walked through the house for the last time. Mom was 63 years old, but I noticed for the first time how old she looked. She was always just 'Mom'--full of love and concern, with a fantastic sense of humor. My four brothers had trained her to be the perfect straight man for all their jokes and she reveled in it. Did I have the right to leave her like this? Would she be here when I returned? I probably wouldn't have felt such guilt had I been drafted, but I had opted for this.

I wouldn't be able to say goodbye to Pop, who was at work, but I could picture him in my mind sitting in his Morris chair reading the N.Y. Times.

I walked into my bedroom. I was the only one in the family who didn't have to share a bed because I was the baby and the only girl.

I never could figure out just what economic bracket my family belonged to. We certainly weren't rich, but I never remembered being hungry or thinking we were poor. I knew we were all living through what was called a 'depression,' but Pop and my older brothers had always had jobs (Pop saw to that.) I never had a lot of money to spend on any fancy clothes, but neither did any of my friends.

We could go to a movie for a dime and see a double feature, cartoon, newsreel and cliffhanger serial, and if we had an extra nickel (and I always did), could buy a big bag of peanuts at Woolworth's.

Every Saturday at 9 a.m., Pop and I would get in a subway, go to the city and spend the day at the Museum of Natural History. We went through it slowly, with Pop explaining everything to me in detail. I thought he was the smartest man in the world because there wasn't a question I would ask that he couldn't answer. We would take a break at noon and go outside where he would buy a nickel apple from one of the men selling them on the street. Pop said they were called 'depression apples.'

After we finished our apple lunch, we would return to the museum and continue our tour. I distinctly remember returning home with him one night just in time for supper. We were all sitting at the table when one of my brothers asked me what I had seen. I dove into detail with great enthusiasm, describing the chicken/egg display that was there. It was a series of egg embryos, each one in progressive development "with a little baby chick inside each one," I excitedly explained.

Mom became furious with Pop for showing me such sexy filth at my tender age. I was a naive twelve-year-old, but figured this must have had something to do with having babies, because Mom was so upset. I had absolutely no idea where babies came from. I thought it possibly had something to do with a man and woman kissing. All my brothers had tears in their eyes from laughing, and the more they laughed, the madder Mom became.

Pop and I continued with our Saturday excursions until I entered high school. After that the trips stopped, but Pop never stopped teaching and loving and caring. He was elated when I passed the entrance exam for Catholic high school, and I know the ten-cent-a-day carfare plus books were an extra financial burden. I could have walked to the neighborhood public high, but my parents wouldn't hear of it.

After high school, tuition for the hospital and nurses' training was $350, plus the cost of uniforms. I know that they had to take out a loan to pay for it. They never complained about the cost, and thank God I had the sense to thank them many times for the sacrifices they made. Yes, I guess we were on the poor side, but I never knew it. I never felt deprived. I knew that there was more love and fun in my home than in the houses of any of my friends.

My husband once told a friend that the members of my family kissed one another goodbye when they were leaving the room to go to the bathroom. That was a slight exaggeration, but I admit there was lots of love and affection.

And now I was leaving all this love and security behind, knowing I would be alone for the first time in my life. When it was time to leave and get the train to Ft. Monmouth, my brother Jack said he would accompany me.

I kissed Mom and Kay goodbye, holding myself in tight reign. When I bent down to kiss my nephew Jackie, he put out his arms and said "Sis" for the first time, and I nearly collapsed. I yelled goodbye and ran out the door. Jack followed me out and said, "You're leaving for overseas--I know all the symptoms." I pulled myself together and dried my tears, happy I had gotten away from Mom without her knowing I was leaving.

On the subway ride to Penn Station, Jack and I had a good discussion about our childhood. We both agreed that we had been lucky kids and had a lot for which to be thankful. I apologized for all the mean things I had done to him when we were little. Pop had a theory that boys didn't hit girls, and I, knowing the theory, abused the hell out of it. Pop often told me of the many times Jack would come staggering into the room with me on his back, pulling his hair, just to prove who was actually causing the trouble.

Jack said he forgave me and took me into a bar at Penn Station for a farewell drink. I ordered a Tom Collins, the drink of the early 40's, and Jack ordered a shot of whiskey. I couldn't believe my ears--he had always been a coffee or coca-cola man. God, I thought sadly, how the Navy has changed him.

He lifted his glass and proposed a toast. "Here's to when we are all safely home again" he said, and then downed the drink in one shot. I was very upset to think that this new habit had become part of his life. My disappointment quickly turned to relief, though, when I saw the distressed expression on his face. He winced and said, "I absolutely hate this crap, but how can you say goodbye to your kid sister with a coke." (Thank you, God.)

He took my hand, looked me in the eye and passed along some words of wisdom. "I wish I could give you lots of good advice," he said, "but all I can do is tell you what Harry (our older brother, also in the Navy) told me: Keep your bowels open, your mouth shut and never, never volunteer." (Too late, Jack.)

Kissing Jack goodbye at the train was the last physical contact I would have with my family for 25 long months. (Every day is like a year, a year whose days are long. Thank you, Oscar Wilde.)

CHAPTER IV

On April 7, 1943, 15 nurses left Ft. Monmouth for Camp Patrick Henry in Virginia, the port of embarkation. We joined up with 35 more nurses to make up the nurse component of the 74th station hospital.

We arrived at Patrick Henry in a thunderstorm and sat in the dark for two hours because no one knew we were coming. I would later learn that this mess-up was S.O.P. (Standard Operating Procedure) for the Army. It was probably occasions like this that gave birth to the Army motto, S.N.A.F.U. (Situation Normal All Fouled Up--censored version.)

The day before embarkation, we were told that there would be a Mass for Catholic personnel in the mess hall. I never saw such a crowd of scared holy people. The place was mobbed and the poor lone priest said that because of the size of the crowd he would have to give "General Absolution" instead of hearing confessions. I was really impressed. I had heard about General Absolution, but never dreamed it would be happening to me. I was a little sorry that I had led such a quiet life because this General Absolution would dump all my sins and I wouldn't even have to tell anybody. I stopped having humorous thoughts when I remembered the nuns in school telling us that it was only done in extreme emergencies. Dear God, I thought, they really expect us to die.

On Mother's Day, we marched in formation to the ship that would take us on our journey. We had no basic training and no idea where we were going. I can still remember that intense, emotional moment as I walked up the gangplank to the ship. I stepped on board, and all I could think of was--"How long, how long?"

We were packed eight in a stateroom and adrenaline was running high as we pulled from port and joined the convoy. No one knew what our final destination would be; we all just hoped we would get there. I think the Navy should have paid me because I spent more time devoted to looking for subs than the sailors who were standing watch.

The only excitement came when we lagged behind the convoy because of some engine trouble. It was frightening to see everyone pulling ahead of us, and it was great to see our Navy escort coming back to check on us from time to time. We caught up with the gang the next day and it was good to be part of the group again. Somewhere in the middle of the trip an announcement was broadcast over the ship's radio that the "hostilities in Africa have ceased."

Someone sighted the Rock of Gibraltar and we finally knew where we were going. The chief nurse didn't think it was funny when I announced to the assembly that the reason Hitler quit was because he found out O'Reilly was landing. She thought it was even less funny when I asked her if we could turn around and go home since the war in Africa was over.

In mid-May, 1944, I landed in North Africa, a spoiled, dependent, unprepared, naive kid who had a lot of growing up to do, and did it in North Africa.

CHAPTER V

Before continuing with the story of my journey to Africa, I would like to explain my philosophy regarding my own ideas and that of the Army. It had a direct bearing on how I responded to different situations during my career and might explain why I struggled so often with issues that did not seem to be as difficult for others to deal with.

All Army nurses are commissioned Second Lieutenants. I heard the reason for this was because in World War I they weren't commissioned, and as a result weren't respected. After much reasoning, the 'powers that be' decided that commissions were in order.

Every old ex-dogface knows that if a man is not respected, his commission will awe no one. The same goes for nurses. If the men don't respect the nurse, they aren't going to be overwhelmingly reverent because of the bars that nurse is wearing. My head nurse told me that I used my bars as "chips on my shoulder," but I honestly felt I functioned better as a nurse without the bars.

Case in point: When I was in Italy they made the Anzio beachhead. At that time we were functioning as a station hospital, taking care of the troops in the replacement depot (the repo depo.) I went to the commanding officer ('old man') and told him I wanted to transfer out to Anzio. He explained to me that the Army would take good care of a man without an arm or a leg, but to really help the war effort, I would better serve the Army if I treated a man with a broken finger who, when healed, could shoot a gun.

The discussion got a little heated and I ended up telling him that he could take care of the man with the finger and give me the man with the missing arm or leg. I guess you could say he won the argument because I never did get my transfer, but that was how I felt. To me, being an Army officer definitely took second place.

I realize now that this philosophy had been ingrained in me from my earliest days of nurses' training. The contrast between my responsibilities as a nurse and responsibilities as an officer would always be diametrically opposed to each other. Later in life the conflict I had always struggled with came to the surface again when I read the following quote by General Omar Bradley from a book on Patton. As I was reading it, the incredible words I had written down while in nurses' training came back to me as well:

Ruth Jones, R.N. - Nursing instructor at Norwegian:	General Omar Bradley:
When you get into uniform to go on duty at the hospital, leave all your worries, troubles and complaints here at the nurses' residence. When you cross the street and enter the hospital, all of your cares, concerns and thoughts should go into the care and comfort of the patients who are under your care. Your life at this time is solely devoted to them.	In time of war the only value that can be fixed to any unit is the tactical value of that unit in winning the war. Even the lives of those men assigned to it become nothing more than the tools to be used in the accomplishment of that mission. War has neither the time nor the heart to concern itself with the individual and the dignity of man. Each day new lives must be spent to pay for the cost of that day's objective.

I still don't understand how anyone could serve these two masters--humanity vs. military--at the same time. I can't comprehend how anyone could reconcile the vast differences between the two.

Getting back to rank, I suppose that in truth, at times I did get a little dramatic. I would tell a guy to lie still so his wounds would heal, then turn away. Two minutes later he would be all over the cot and I would have to go back and yell at him again. "Yes, Ma'am," he would say--"You're an officer." I would tell him that, no, it was not an order, it was just good advice, nurse to patient. He would say "Yes, Lieutenant," so I would take off my bar, pin it on his shirt and say, "Now I'm a nurse. Lie still." I guess I did it a lot, because one day I found myself down to only one bar.

Like everything I did in the Army, this backfired on me. One day in Italy the chaplain came up to me as I was getting off duty and said he had a jeep and was going into Naples. He asked if I wanted to join him. I ran into the chief nurse's tent and asked the Captain for permission to go along.

Standing tall, with eyebrows arched and nostrils flaring, she said that I absolutely could go, and hoped I would even have a good time. But, she continued, I would have to do so in a Class A uniform, and would have to do it without borrowing a single bar from anyone in the outfit. She then asked if I could do that.

I knew I couldn't do it. So did she. Class A uniform was a blouse with two bars--one more than I possessed. I went to my tent, got some lire and asked Chappie to get me some bars at the P.X. Walking back to my tent, I remembered that she had reprimanded me about this bad habit a couple of times. I think that was the day I stopped illegally commissioning enlisted men.

Perhaps if I had had to work hard for a commission it would have meant more to me. All I wanted to do was to be a good nurse.

Another night in Africa, I had a patient who was a Major and had to go to X-ray the following morning. I told Hugo, my ward man, to give him a cleansing enema. Every time I passed Hugo during the night I would ask him if he had done it, and every time Hugo would say no--that the Major would have it at his convenience, not at the private's (Hugo's) convenience. Now really, how much of this crap could Hugo and I take. I went to the tent and told the Major that unless he had that gold leaf tattooed on his shoulder, he would have an enema now, and the lowly private would give it. I told him if it was not done in half an hour a 2nd Lieutenant, namely me, would do it.

Hugo gave it. The next day one of the doctors told me that the Major, in a rage, had come storming into the rec tent where the Colonel was and told him about this disrespectful 2nd Lieutenant nurse. The doctor said I would have been proud of the old man. He told the Major that if the 2nd Lieutenant's name was O'Reilly, he had best have the corpsman give the enema, as she surely would have--and it probably would have been an "HHH" (high, hot and a hell of a lot).

I guess I was never really rank-conscious. One night at Ft. Monmouth, after returning from overseas, I had been standing in mess line and got into trouble again. An ambulatory patient in uniform (another Major) was standing in line in front of me. He started really feeling up the nurse in front of him, running his hands up and down her body, and she told him to knock it off. "Oh," he said to her, "you can tell you haven't been overseas."

I tapped him on the shoulder and asked him what he meant by that. He told me that he had been overseas and the nurses over there all loved that sort of thing. "Well," I screamed, "here's a nurse (1st Lieutenant now) who was overseas and if you lay a finger on me you'll find yourself on the floor." He slinked away without another word.

Later that night, I was acting night supervisor and had the evening off. As I was walking across the parade ground to go to a movie, I saw him and a fellow officer approaching. I heard him say, "Here she is now," so I knew he had been talking about me. I casually walked past him without saluting (an unheard of thing in a chicken outfit like Ft. Monmouth where 2nd Lieutenants saluted 1st Lieutenants). "Stop," he screamed. I turned and he said, "We salute superior officers on this post." I looked at the man, not the uniform, told him to go to hell and walked on. I left him standing with his mouth open.

I may have looked cool but was really dying inside. I went to the movie, but only stayed about half an hour. I couldn't concentrate on what I was watching. I returned to the barracks, took a real hot bath and laid awake all night. This is it, I thought--big trouble. This place was nothing like my old outfit, where I had always been able to get away with so much.

I got up at seven and hid all day in the P.X. At 7 p.m. I went on duty and, because I was night supervisor, had to get the report from the head nurse herself. I came through the door waving a white handkerchief--might as well make light of it, I thought--Dear God, get me out of this mess. She told me that the commanding officer had come storming into her office demanding to know who the flaming asshole 1st Lieutenant was who told a Major to go to hell. To cover me, she told him she thought I had a little "battle fatigue," but I think the thing that really saved me was the fact that I had just gotten the officers ward to pass inspection for the first time in four weeks.

I was also a hero because about a week before that I had disarmed a G.I. who was holding a group at gunpoint. The real truth of the story is that one of the nurses called to tell me a patient had just come back from a pass, was very drunk and was holding a gun on the nurse and corpsman on the E.E.N.T. (Eye, Ear, Nose and Throat) ward.

I was really upset because I had been in charge of that ward before becoming night supervisor. They had already called the O.D. (Officer of the Day) and when I got there I found quite a large group looking at the guy with the gun. All I really saw, though, was this Sergeant with his broken jaw hanging open. All I could think of was the tremendous amount of time and effort he and I had spent cleaning and irrigating his wired jaw. I pushed the gun aside, not really being aware of it, so I could see just how much damage he had done to himself. There was nothing heroic about it, but what the hell--no harm in having people think you are brave. Anyway, the chief nurse covered for me with the C.O. I think the fact that she herself had spent two years overseas influenced her decision. She didn't even yell.

I remember there was one thing that I did respect, if not rank. One day, walking down a street in Naples, I was stopped by two G.I.s who were walking behind me. "Lieutenant," one said, "we are baffled. We have been following you for three blocks and we can't figure out who you are saluting. We know it's not rank because you are saluting enlisted men, but not all enlisted men, so what goes?"

I looked at their shirts and saw that they were wearing the infantryman's badge--a silver rifle on a blue background. I saluted them and they understood immediately. They returned the salute, smiled and said, "Thank you."

I know that Winston Churchill was speaking of the British Air Force when he said, "Never has so much been done by so few," but to me that famous quote stands for the Infantrymen of the United States Army.

I can't tell you how much I loved and respected the infantrymen. They were always the heroes of the war in my eyes. They appreciated every little thing a nurse would do to make their lives a little better. They cheered me up much more than I possibly could have done to help them.

One day I was working the officer's ward, doing dressings and medications. I started off with the first bed and went straight up the line. Everyone was laughing and talking and in good spirits as I approached the fourth patient. He was a Captain who had a sour puss and a morose disposition. I tried some light talk on him but nothing seemed to work. He persisted in being grumpy. I asked him how he made it into the infantry because he was nothing like any other 'dogface' I had ever met. All the fellows started screaming that he was not infantry. "Well," I replied, "He's got a bullet in his butt that I just put a dressing on--where did that come from?"

"He was shot by one of his own men," they all bellowed. They apparently didn't want any part of the guy. "We were taught to be leaders of men," a very young 2nd Lieutenant exclaimed. Suddenly everyone stopped, and I thought that the young officer who uttered that statement surely must have had a complete loss of sanity. Didn't he realize that he was sitting in the midst of officers from all corps--ordinance, artillery, signal and so forth? All these warriors considered themselves leaders of men.

By the time he realized his mistake it was a too late, and the discussion that followed--infantry vs. the rest of the Army--lasted until time for mess. And after all was said and done, these leaders didn't sound any different to me, in either logic or bravado (B.S.), than the young kids they were leading.

That particular argument ended peacefully, but I remember a couple that took a bad turn.

One day I was sitting on the side of his bed, taking care of a patient. The guy in the next bed, right alongside of me, was laying on his bunk having a discussion with another patient who was standing at the foot of his bed. They were arguing the merits and faults of Frank Sinatra. I was listening carefully because I could tell it was starting to heat up--with Frank it was either a case of love or hate. The guy laying in the bed said to the guy standing at his feet, "Well, I personally think that Frankie is a fag and if you love him so much, you . . ."

I knew what the end of the sentence was going to be and, in order to prevent mayhem, threw myself on top of the guy lying down. The fellow at the foot, also knowing what the rest of the sentence was going to be, threw himself on the bed and landed on top of me. All the other guys started to scream and the three of us tumbled off the cot and onto the floor sandwich-style, with me being the meat.

I was a little annoyed because with the kind of luck I usually had, this would be the precise moment the C.O. making rounds would catch me rolling around on the floor in the midst of it all. I started yelling, "at ease!" and everyone really quieted down. Fortunately, we didn't get caught and we all got away without any difficulty. I was also spared the usual sermon about my being too soft and for running my tents with a lack of discipline. I heard that a lot.

Another situation that caused many arguments was the board game, Monopoly. Every single time a patient borrowed that game from the Red Cross and brought into the ward, there was a fight--not just an argument, but a real, live drawn-out fight. It happened every time, even though the cast of players changed over the weeks and months, because they were all young kids and all played the game the same way. I finally made a rule that they were not permitted to bring the game into any of the three tents I was in charge of. The kids kept saying that I was not being a good mother because they were all being punished for something some other kid had done. I thought I should give in and relented when they promised they would not fight.

The game came in and it started off nice and quiet. It proceeded to get louder and louder--different patients but the same age bracket of 17 and 18 year olds. Every game went the same way. One guy would pull away from the group by making some advantageous real estate deals. He would then buy off everybody in financial difficulty with large amounts of play money and would start getting a big head and start boasting. Then the game would turn the corner. Instead of the guy with the most money winning the game, the aim changed to beat 'loud mouth' into submission. All the players who had less money than the 'Captain of Industry' would sell off their stuff to one guy who would then suddenly become the new leader.

It was when the dishonest stuff started that the fights always started. Yells of "that's not fair" began when one loser would sell the other loser a set of railroads for $10, spurning the big winner's offer of hundreds. Many, many, many times the game would end in a fistfight, and I would have to take it away again. I couldn't punish anyone by sending them to their beds or to their room, and the timeout method wasn't to come into disciplinary rules for many years. Nevertheless, I warned them that the day would come when they would understand the grief they were causing me. I told them to remember that moment and to think of me when they went through the ordeal of playing Monopoly with their own kids.

The kids would argue over anything and everything. On several occasions, patients sketched pictures of me on V mail so I could send them home to my parents. The kids always passed the artwork around, criticizing them like they were expensive portraits. They would comment each time on everything--the nose was too big or too small, the chin not long enough to too long. Anything for a fight.

CHAPTER VI

Getting back to my trip to Africa: I had a good spot on the rail to watch disembarkation of the troops. First off was a detachment of WACS. They walked down the gangplank, climbed into trucks and were driven away. So far, so good. Next, the nurses got off. We stood on the dock in formation. We waited while one truck was loaded with our barracks bags and bedrolls. We continued to stand in formation with musette bags and gas masks, waiting to see what would happen next. Damned if we didn't wind up having to march about two miles (which seemed like ten) to Goat Hill. I don't know how it came by that name. I didn't see any goats, so it must have been the way it smelled.

It was an area of tents. No cots. Nothing but tents. Empty tents. We all screamed, wanting to know what happened to the WACS. It didn't help our morale any when we learned that the WACS were going to be stationed at a hotel in Oran. We were told to grow up and stop complaining.

Goat Hill turned out to be a time of cold C Rations, dust storms, helmet baths, sleeping on the ground and the worst situation of all--the outdoor latrine. I am sure that somewhere in the Pentagon there is a 12-page book of procedures dealing exclusively with the construction of the latrine, but they all looked and smelled the same to me.

Four sticks about seven feet long were hammered into the ground. A hunk of canvas was nailed to them, forming a square area. There was no roof. If it was raining we just got wet. Inside the enclosure a deep pit was dug into the ground, topped by a wooden bench with holes carved into the top. I don't know if they got all the flies from supplies, but every latrine I ever saw was equipped with an overwhelming number of them.

My future husband, Jim Allen, was with the engineering outfit that set up our latrine when we moved to Mateur. The cutouts in the bench were so large we had to hold on with both hands. Not only were they extra large, but each one had a name painted over it. Jim told me later that the Colonel complained that he lost an average of two nurses a week down the hole. Jim also said that he told the Colonel the cutouts were custom made only after they had seen the nurses. I don't believe he really said that because at the time Jim was a 1st Lieutenant and, unlike myself, very rank conscious.

The latrines at Goat Hill, however, were my very first experience and I couldn't believe they were for real. I almost wished I had been back at sea, standing in line to use the head. There must have been a shortage of disinfectant, because gasoline was poured into the hole as a deodorant. There was also a notice hung on the door flap warning everyone not to smoke, since the latrines were known to blow up on occasion.

Nothing in my life had prepared me for using one. I remember sitting outside one in the grass, telling a buddy that as desperately as I needed to, I couldn't gather enough courage or stomach to go inside. I thought that my short-lived Army life would dramatically end when I would surely die of autointoxication.

A week later found me sitting on one of the "thrones" (they were four-seaters), calmly discussing the Army, politics and all sorts of mundane things with anyone sitting next to me. I guess this proves how adaptable the human species can be to its environment.

Until cots were issued, we slept on the ground on top of our bedrolls. A bedroll is a piece of canvas about seven feet long upon which we would place our two blankets plus most of our clothes. When we weren't using it as a mattress, we would roll it all up and tie it with a strap.

It went everywhere we went. Some G.I.s had come along and told us that the ground would be softer if we broke up the soil under it. I did this and found that the only thing I accomplished was to put sharp points on all of the rocks, making a bad situation worse. Sleep then became almost impossible.

Jim and I had an ongoing argument for about 35 years on whether or not I had ever been issued a hatchet. He claimed that he had never gotten one and "if the engineers weren't issued a hatchet, you can be damn sure the nurses didn't get one." I distinctly remember having one but could never prove it. He would constantly revive this argument while sitting at the dinner table, surrounded by our nine children. I told him he was obsessed by the discussion because it was the only argument we ever had that he actually had a chance of winning. I think I was supposed to give in on this issue because by that time he was a Lieutenant Colonel in the Army reserve and there weren't too many of us who could, or would, tell the Colonel he was wrong about anything pertaining to the Army.

About a week after we arrived at Goat Hill we received cots and mosquito netting. This was a great improvement. I settled into my cot one night and tucked the netting in all around me. I thought I had killed all the flying insects that were locked in with me but I must have missed a pregnant female. When I woke up the next morning there were about eight buzzing around and I was covered with bites. I was convinced that the only things that thrived in North Africa were mosquitoes and flies--certainly not me.

We had running water. About 100 yards from our tents there was a large water tank and we would grab our helmets and run and get it--(Army humor).

Morning baths were done in a helmet of cold water. All of us would wash our faces first, then arms and legs, leaving our dirty feet until last. When finished, we would dunk our undies and socks in the now dirty water, wring them out and slap them on top of the tent. The intense heat would dry them in about one hour. The days were hot, yet at night we needed a blanket to sleep.

I felt really deprived about this bathing in a helmet business until I realized that the poor guys had to shave with the same helmet of water. I often wondered where the guys fit the shave into the procedure; surely not before washing their face, and double surely not after washing their feet. Too bad Jim and I had spent so much time arguing about the hatchet--he could have settled that question for me.

We were happy when the cots and mosquito netting arrived. Sleeping at night became easier, but trying to keep clean was difficult.

Water was delivered to the area by big tank trucks. There were three buckets for the 50 of us to share. They held much more water than our helmets, so if we waited to get a bucket we could also wash our hair. If anyone was impatient they could take a helmet full, but that would be their wash water for the day. Most of us waited for the buckets to become available.

I was waiting my turn to get a bucket and saw one of the nurses walking toward the tanker with two buckets. I asked her what was going on. She said she had waited for another bucket to be emptied so she could have more water to wash her long hair. Apparently, her reply made total sense to her.

I waited for someone to jump up and grab one of the pails out of her hand and was amazed when everyone became mute and paralyzed. I know that the meek shall inherit the earth, but I didn't want the earth. All I wanted was the bucket. I ran up to her and grabbed the pail. She held on tight but I pulled and started to speak to her softly as I would a sweet, spoiled child. That didn't work for either of us. She thought that I was giving in. I thought that she was going crazy, perhaps from too much sun.

I pulled the pail harder, looked her square in the eye and told her if she did not let go of the pail she would not have any hair on her head left to wash. I threatened to pull out every damn strand she had. I must have looked frightening because she let go of the bucket and I pulled it free. "See," I smiled, "now we both have one. That is good, no?" I went and washed myself, hair and all, then gave the bucket to the next person in line.

We had no choice but to wash our hair at the camp. Orders were given that we could not, under any circumstances, go into Oran to get our hair done. Unfortunately, one of the nurses sneaked out of camp and went to a local beauty salon. When she washed her hair again back at camp, the chlorine turned it a purplish-green, and she had to walk around that way until she finally received some dye from her family and was able to fix it.

During my confrontation with the long-haired nurse, Marty our assistant head nurse, told me that she and the chief had been sitting on the hill smoking a cigarette and had been watching the whole thing from the time the fracas began. She said the chief nurse started to get up, thinking there was going to be a fight that she would need to break up. Marty said she told the chief that it was the beginning of a long era and that she should let people work problems out for themselves or she would forever be involved in breaking up fights.

Marty then added that she was sure I was going to give my comrade a hit in the nose because "just last night you told me how your brothers taught you to make a fist correctly before you were two years old." This is true. I learned not to make the mistake that most girls do of turning in their thumbs before throwing a punch. (Thanks for that very useful hint, brothers!)

About a week before we left the staging area a shower was set up. It was just like the latrine except for the ditch-- there wasn't any. The mud was semi-solid. The shower consisted of a pipe with four holes in it where the cold water came out. I don't know why we were expected to do everything in fours, but the latrine was a four-seater and the shower held four bodies. Our sleeping tents held four cots. I don't think I would have been happy with more than three nude bodies to look at in the shower. I wasn't overly modest, but unlike classical impressionists, I also didn't think that the body, sans clothing, was that great to look at. Let's be honest--most gals don't look like Venus DeMilo.

The only available food was cold C Rations, but one day three of us took a walk and found a detachment of troops who were getting ready for the invasion of Sicily (we didn't know they were going until later.) Every night we would go there to eat because they had hot food and would share it with us. We never told the rest of the gang about it because we knew we had a good thing going and didn't want to blow it.

Before leaving Camp Patrick Henry we were told that we might have trouble getting cigarettes, so we all brought a lot with us. Because of the fear of running out, I also brought a pipe and a couple of packages of Rum and Maple tobacco. Every night after dinner I would light up the pipe and puff away. I thought I was cool. About a year later, after I had become a real experienced veteran, it came back to haunt me. One day in Italy I walked into one of my ward tents and a guy yelled, "Hey, I know you. You're the nurse in Africa who smoked the pipe." I tried to deny that I would ever do such a thing, but I guess my face gave me away. All the guys started calling me Mammy Yocum. We never did have a shortage of cigarettes and I was sorry because I really enjoyed that pipe.

The day finally came when we were to meet up with our doctors and enlisted men. The Fighting 74th was finally getting assembled. Action at last!

The head nurse told us we were also finally going to get a hot meal. To most of the girls, that seemed to be the best part of the deal. We took a long walk over the hill and came upon a group of tents exactly like our setup on Goat Hill.

All of the guys were sitting on the ground anxiously waiting to see what we looked like. We sat down and were mixing it up real friendly-like when the Sergeant said it was time to eat. I couldn't believe my eyes when one of our administration officers handed me a can of cold beans. I guess I looked surprised because he asked if anything was wrong. I told him I thought we were going to get hot food. "Oh," he asked, with a smirk on his face, "would you like it hot?"

Like an innocent fool I answered "Yes." He threw a package of matches at me and said, "Here--heat it up." Everybody laughed and I felt instant hate. I served with that clown for almost two years and never got past being able to just about tolerate him. When I dislike, I really dislike.

I stood there with my face hanging out and determined on the spot that they--all, everybody--would never laugh at me again; with me, I hoped, many times, but never again at me. That was the moment that I grew up in Africa.

I think that some good characteristics worth developing are to become moderately independent and to be able to function all alone. But like most things I did, I carried it to extremes. Today I have nine children and the biggest fault they find with me is my independent nature. What was self-preservation for me in Africa became an attitude of strong will in real life. Every time one of my 24 grandchildren or nine great grandchildren show a little streak of stubbornness or self-will, I get blamed for supplying the genes that caused the problem.

One good thing about that day was that I also met Sergeant Leo. I had used my canteen many times to take a drink in the past, but had never bothered with the cup because all we usually had was powered lemonade and I preferred plain water. On that particular day, we were going to have hot coffee so I needed to use the metal cup that was attached to the bottom of the canteen. I had no idea how to attach the handle that would secure it sufficiently to hold it steady. I was struggling with it when a Sergeant came over and showed me how to do it properly. I thanked him profusely.

About five minutes later I got in line and put out my cup to get some hot coffee. When the mess Sergeant poured the coffee into it, the cup completely collapsed. The hot coffee burned my hand and ran down my pants leg. I looked into the eyes of the mess Sergeant and kind of yelled, "Some damn fool Sergeant just fixed this cup for me." His eyes dilated and I realized that I was yelling at the same Sergeant who had originally fixed the cup. I shouted at him, "It was you!" while he simultaneously shouted, "It was me!" Then we both laughed like all hell and bonded instantly.

He told me that his name was Leo and he was the first enlisted man in the outfit that I met. He became our mess Sergeant and from that day on he called me nothing but Sarge, and I called him Cookie. When I like, I really like.

Looking back on it, the only exciting thing that happened on Goat Hill was the night I thought we were bombed. We were all asleep in our tents when a terrible noise woke me at about 3 a.m. I couldn't breathe because something very heavy was lying on my face. I was sure I had heard the sound of airplanes. I lifted my arms, but my body was completely covered with canvas. There wasn't a sound in the tent, and I thought everyone was dead.

Finally I heard someone say, "What the hell happened" and I thanked God that someone besides myself was still alive. I heard a man's voice say, "Let's get them out" and struggled to free myself so I could go give first aid to the wounded. I felt like a real jerk when I managed to crawl out from under everything and discovered the problem. The center pole holding up the tent had snapped, causing it to collapse on us. I didn't tell a soul that I thought it was 'enemy action,' and smiled when the guard said he was real proud of us because no one had screamed during our ordeal. Of course, the Army came up with a clever way to solve our problem--they told all of us to simply move to the middle of the tent.

Monotony was broken the second week of June when ten of us were sent on detached service. We were sent to a general hospital to relieve a group of nurses who had been

He looked at me like I had just dropped in from another planet and said indignantly, "Who the hell are you?"

"I, sir, am the damn fool who called you, evidently mistaken in thinking we were both on duty."

Marty kept kicking me under the table, but I was really pissed and wouldn't back off. "We just got here from stateside," she said to placate the Captain, "and we have a lot to learn."

I did have a lot to learn. For instance, I found out the procedure I should have followed that night was that, except in cases of emergency (certainly not cramps), I should have done whatever I thought was necessary without having an order. The next time I saw the doctor, who worked the ward with me, I would make sure to get the written order to cover any procedure I may have done. This is known in the Army as 'covering your ass' and I am sure it still holds true today in the Army, Navy, Air Force and Marines and probably for every underling in any civilian occupation in the good old U.S.A.

When we left the mess tent, I got a long sermon from Marty about--what else--rank, and how we must show self-control with superior officers. Poor Marty. She was great and I loved her dearly. I'm sure I caused her a lot of unintentional grief.

Thank God our outfit was different. Perhaps it was because we all started out together practically as civilians, who then grew together in wisdom and age (though maybe some of us were not as strong in the wisdom department.) The only time I ever got in trouble was when I was on detached service and away from my Army family.

Two weeks later we were all called back to Goat Hill and were put on alert. At last we were going to start functioning as the Fighting 74th.

CHAPTER VII

The first week of July the good news came. We were finally going to set up the 74th station hospital. We were all excited about getting an outfit of our own. We were going to take care of the casualties from the Sicilian Invasion-- double jeopardy for the poor guys who would need our tender loving care. We had lots of love, but none of us had any experience.

I realize that fighting a war is a difficult task for Command, but in reality this move was like something out of a Keystone Comedy. I know that the movement of personnel and equipment is a major logistical problem and also know that it's easy to sit on the sidelines and criticize, but this was too much.

We, along with all our gear, were packed into trucks and taken to the train station for embarkation. We were told that the trip across Africa would probably take six or seven days. When I looked at the engine I thought it would be a miracle if it even got out of the station. The train looked nothing like anything I had ever seen in Grand Central or Penn Station. Coming from Brooklyn, it was the only source of reference I had.

Each car was broken up into about eight compartments. Each compartment had two benches, one facing the other, each with a window. I don't know how many passengers it would normally carry in peacetime, but for our use each compartment was packed with six bodies. At night we slept two on each bench and two on the floor. There was a little sink that we were ordered not to use, so we only washed when the train stopped for a water fill.

After about two days out it started to smell real gamey. There was also no dining car, so for six days we ate cold K or C rations. Every time we pulled into a siding we would pray that a British Army train would pull up next to us. Whenever we encountered them, we would stick our canteen cups out the window, and the Tommies would fill them up with hot tea. It was the best food we had for six days.

Only two orders were issued to us as we settled in. First we were not, under any circumstances, to get off the train. Secondly, we were not to eat any native food, and could only have what would be issued to us--C or K rations. Before the train reached its destination in Mateur six days later, I had disobeyed both orders. In the sixty some odd years since the end of Archie Bunker's Big W.W. II, I have heard many hilarious and unbelievable stories of what some G.I.s did and got away with during their Army lives. But not me. I always got caught.

The second day out, the chaplain asked me if I wanted to ride in the engine cab with him. I received an O.K. from the chief nurse and couldn't believe my good luck. The heat inside the train was unbearable, but it was cool inside the cab. I rode in that cab for about five hours until we pulled into a siding and I decided to go back to my compartment.

To my amazement, none of my buddies would let me in. They gave me a mirror so that I could see myself. I couldn't believe how dirty I had become. I dug a towel out of my musette bag and used the water in my canteen to try to clean myself up. They wouldn't share their precious water with me, so I did a real half-assed job. They were all peeved at me, speaking only to say obscene things.

The good thing about not being allowed into my compartment was that I got to sit on the steps with a couple of our doctors. I asked them if their group had ostracized them too. They told me the reason they were riding the steps was because they had run out of money and the other guys would not let them play cards on credit. I think one of the reasons these guys charged so much for an office visit when they returned stateside was to make up for the money they had lost playing cards during the war.

We continued on for a couple of hours and then pulled into a siding, where a group of Arabs was selling fruit. My so-called friends, who were in the train, handed two helmets out to me and said to get them some grapes. I thought this might be a good opportunity to get back in their good graces and back into the compartment, so I decided to hell with the orders. I jumped off the steps where I was sitting and filled up the two helmets. I couldn't believe my eyes when I saw the train starting to pull away.

The only thing my so-called buddies cared about were the grapes. None of them were the least bit concerned that the train was starting to pull away and I was still standing there on foreign soil. They kept yelling, "Throw the grapes, Mick, throw the grapes!" While they were shouting, I could just picture myself stranded in an Arabian market somewhere in North Africa. I ran alongside the car holding up the grapes, and they leaned out the window and grabbed the helmets. No one reached for me. The grapes were the priority of the day.

Thank God one of the surgeons with a fast mind grabbed me and pulled me aboard. He must have reminded me at least twice a week after that experience that the only reason I was still with the outfit was because of his quick wits. After a couple of months I told him that I probably would have been better off if he had left me in the Arabian market--that being in a harem couldn't have been any worse than our setup. One day a patient asked me if the doctor was my father, because he used to tell everyone in the tent that "Mickey wouldn't be here if it weren't for me." He would never explain the statement, he would just make it.

I was glad to be back on the train again, but now instead of my comrades being displeased with me, I was infuriated with them. They turned my wrath into love by telling me that the old man and chief nurse didn't know I had gotten off the train, but threatened that they would tell all if I didn't forgive and forget. I found out later that both my bosses did know about my escapade. They just figured that the scare I got did more good than any disciplinary action they could have taken. One good thing about my being a 2nd Lieutenant was that they couldn't demote me because the next step down would have been to civilian, and what would they do with a civilian in North Africa?

I had heard that there were a few fistfights in the enlisted men's cars. We didn't have any physical disagreements in the nurses' cars; however, there was much moaning and groaning. It would be difficult for anyone who wasn't there to imagine what it was like to be locked up together for six days. No one had a radio, so we didn't even have music to "soothe the savage beast."

The eminent medical profession had not yet discovered PMS (Pre-Menstrual Syndrome), so we didn't have a scientific name for what was really driving all of us crazy. I don't think it would have helped even if we had been able to put a name on it. Sum it up: 53 miserable females.

The Great Train Movement ended after six days without any casualties. We disembarked from the train and were driven to where we would set up our hospital. When we arrived, I jumped off the truck and did a 360-degree turn. There was not one single structure, or any sign of life, as far as the eye could see.

CHAPTER VIII

Everyone went to work as we began to set up our new home in North Africa. It would be the location where we would treat the casualties from Sicily. The enlisted men did all of the manual labor involved in assembling the structure of the hospital, which was mostly composed of tents.

The ward tents, which housed the patients, were big, long and narrow and held about 18 cots. They were set in the center of the compound. Tents for X-Ray, E.E.N.T. (Eye, Ear, Nose and Throat), dental, and the operating room were in Quonset huts, prefabricated so they could be pulled down and then reassembled in a hurry. These huts were located on one side of the ward tents. Tents for supply, motor pool, pharmacy and mail were located on the other side of the ward tents. There were two large mess tents for the ambulatory patients, to the side of the ward tents. The mess tents for the enlisted men and one for the officers were located near the patients' mess. The personnel tents, where we slept, were located on the periphery of the hospital site.

Two large ward tents were attached and made into one big one. This was called a recreational area and became known as a rec tent. There were three rec tents, one for patients run by the Red Cross workers, and one each for officers and enlisted men. The procedure was for the men to set up the hospital first and then the area of personnel sleeping tents. Before any enlisted men or officers' tents were raised, however, the two designated rec tents were put up. Everyone thought that was great because we would rather have a place to meet and gripe than have a place to sleep. We hadn't finished setting up our rec tents before we received our first patients. We were all ready for them because we had been assigned our tents the minute they were erected, so the beds were up and we were ready to start our 'TLC.'

The wounds were a variety of shrapnel and bullets. All the men carried packs of sulfur powder that they would pour into their own wounds or their buddy's wounds. Surprisingly enough, we had very few fatalities.

African weather was nothing like anything I had experienced in Brooklyn. The days were unbearably hot and we had to sleep with two blankets at night. If we wanted a drink we obtained it from lister bags, which were scattered all over the area. These were canvas bags containing water that had a ratio, I am sure, of two parts chlorine to one part water. During the day the temperature of the water must have been over 100 degrees. It was actually hot to drink.

Everyone was getting dehydrated from the scarcity of fluids, so the old man solved the problem by filling up the huge metal water canisters with African vino. What a difference that made. No one complained anymore about being thirsty. As a matter of fact, I remember seeing about eight of the guys marching in formation "hut-twoing" right out of the camp, all of them in perfect step--backwards.

CHAPTER IX

Of all the good memories of the war, the best and most pleasant were of the patients. What an unbelievable bunch of guys.

One time I was writing a letter home for one of the patients who was not able to do it for himself. He was telling his mother that he had been shot in the arm. I looked at him with amazement because he didn't have an arm. When I remarked that he would surely have to tell her the truth at some point he said, "Yes, but I'm going to do it in stages. First I'll tell her I've been shot. Then it's infected. Then I might have to lose it. Then I'll tell her I did lose it. Then it won't be such a shock to her--she'll get it in degrees." Imagine, here was a guy without an arm, whose biggest worry was how to spare his mother any anxiety.

In August the heat became intolerable. We would perspire profusely and then the dust on our legs would turn to mud and there was never enough water. The food was bad and the flies were everywhere.

I would be freezing at night, get up at 6 a.m., wash in a helmet and occasionally would go on duty in a mean, cantankerous mood. Then I would enter their tents, and would be greeted by a bunch of smiling faces wishing me a happy "Good morning!" When I would ask them how they could be so happy, they would simply reply that "we're still alive."

It made the list of inconveniences that I had been griping about seem very insignificant. So I would stop griping and instead of feeling sorry for myself, I would thank God that I was in a position that enabled me to be there. I often thought about all the mothers, wives, sisters and sweethearts who would have given anything they possessed to be in my place. I wasn't the only one who felt that way. Every nurse in the outfit had the same feelings.

It was during this period that I shed tears for the second time. I later wrote home about it: "...Yesterday I celebrated my 6th month anniversary as an Army nurse. Ironically enough on that day I lost my first case. Last night I felt so discouraged and unhappy that I was sorry I had ever gotten into this mess. I couldn't understand what was the matter with me. I have had many patients die during my three years at the Norwegian Hospital. I know I am not cold or hard, but I should be used to death by this time. But yesterday was so different. I worked so hard on him. It seems so terrible to think that he had lasted so long, had gone through so much and yet to no good. He was a young kid from down south, so sweet and quiet and I had grown so fond of him. He died holding my hand. He thought he was going to sleep. He made me promise to give him an alcohol sponge when he woke up, but he never woke up..." That was a tough day I'll never forget.

Fortunately, though, there were also fun things happening too. It was the rainy season then, and patients would make little ditches running from one end of the tent to the other. After construction was completed and the water was high enough, a patient in the first bed would make a little boat, fold up a message, and send it on its way. A patient further down the line would give that boat a little push, sometimes adding to the message. This would continue until the boat arrived at the end of the waterway, where the 'point man' would turn it around and send it back with a new message. I think some of the communications were dirty, because there were a lot that they wouldn't let me read. I only got to read the funny ones.

I considered this a form of occupational therapy, but it didn't go over too well with the chief nurse. She liked to see all the cots lined up in a straight line. I also pulled the cots out of line so the bed patients could play cards. All the fun and games created kind of a messy-looking tent, but the kids in my tent were happy.

I wrote home one day: "...Things here are much the same. Some days we are so busy we can't take a minute to rest. Other times we are so slow we almost go backwards. Today is one of those days. Very slow. I am on duty now. I have all the beds pulled out of line so the fellows that can't get out of bed can play cards together. If the boss comes in she will lay me out good and proper. But my babes are happy, and that's all that counts. Your little daughter will never get a promotion. I think I may be broken to a civilian, but I think contentment is three quarters of the treatment these boys need. Guess it is about time I signed off and did some nursing around here. Besides, there is an argument about the card game and I have to shut them up or else..."

During the day we would roll up the sides of the tents so that the guys who weren't ambulatory could see what was going on outside. They used to lie on their cots and watch the Arab families passing by. The Arab men would always be riding on a camel or a donkey, while the females in the family would follow behind, carrying large bundles on their heads and children in their arms. All the fellows thought that that was a wonderful idea and said they were going to initiate the concept when they got home after the war. I don't think their plan ever got off the ground (thank God.) I never did see it when I returned stateside.

It was a wonderful place to be though. As I wrote home: "...What a riot this place is. I am working in ward 8 today. It is supposed to be a ward for psychiatric patients but thank God we don't have any, so it is filled up with medical cases. The fellows all know what kind of patients are supposed to be in here, so all they do all day is clown around, acting like nuts. One makes believe he is the President and calls me Eleanor. Another one lays in bed all day making up songs about the war and nurses. The President has just finished a speech to Congress. Right in the middle of it, the climax, he stopped and walked out with the remark that he had to go fishing. Every time the ambulance goes by they all run to the back of the tents yelling, "There's an ambulance, someone must be sick." I have to stop. It's impossible to write. The fellas all say that I am being paid to take care of them. General McArthur, General Eisenhower and the Secretary of State just came in. In about five more minutes I am going to put the whole lot of them in straightjackets…"

One day we received a message from command headquarters that a farmer in our area complained that some of our patients had been stealing his grapes. We received a form from our old man directing all ward officers (who were doctors) to investigate this charge and to take immediate disciplinary action against anyone found guilty of this crime.

My ward officer was a great guy. He asked for all those who had been stealing grapes to raise their hands. Every ambulatory patient did so. He had all of them assemble outside the tents, looked at his watch, and told them to stand at attention. After one minute he told them to be at ease and initialed the memorandum stating that disciplinary action had been taken. Then we all proceeded to eat the stolen grapes. Doctors don't make any better soldiers than nurses do!

CHAPTER X

I received a letter from my brother, Harry, who was a Lieutenant in the Navy. After inquiring about my health and welfare he assured me that I had nothing to fear from the Germans because he and the United States Navy had the Mediterranean Sea secured. I didn't know what specific part of the Med he was talking about, because his letter arrived in the last batch of mail we were to receive for a couple of weeks.

Supplies were scarce, so I was surprised when the chief nurse told me to go to the supply tent to pick up a raincoat. I had been issued a new uniform, but my dress trench coat had not yet arrived. When I got to supply, there were a bunch of smiling boys who told me they had one just my size, all ready for me to wear. I grabbed the coat, thanked them and returned to my tent to try it on.

The coat trailed on the ground as I walked and the sleeves were a good 12-15 inches past my wrists. I quickly ran back to the supply tent, and told the same group I needed a smaller one. They said they had given me the smallest one on hand. Then they burst into laughter. I found out later that they had been waiting to see my reaction to the fit. Apparently it made their day. I knew it would be useless to argue with them, so I decided to let them have their laughs and went straight to the top.

I knew the old man was inspecting the tents with the head nurse, so I put the coat on and stood at the flap of the first tent to meet him as he exited. When he came out I threw him a real military salute and the sleeve of the coat snapped around my head, blinding my view. The bottom of the coat was three inches in the mud. The Colonel returned the salute with a rather startled look on his face, but proceeded to enter the next tent to the command of "Attention!"

I quickly ran to the exit of that tent and was standing there, waiting for him again as he came out. I threw another salute and the coat once again whipped itself around my head. The startled look came back upon his face. "OK, O'Reilly, why are you so salute happy?" I explained that the coat had just been issued to me and I couldn't possibly wear it. He said to get a smaller one. I told him that apparently this was the smallest coat on hand.

"Can I perhaps make it fit by using scissors?" I asked. "No, you can't mutilate government property. It's not your coat." End of discussion.

So I rolled up the sleeves, taped up the hem (I wasn't allowed to use pins either), and wore that stupid raincoat for three weeks until my issue arrived.

Then things started to get a little tough and we really started to rough it. There was a shortage of everything. We had no coffee and had to drink powdered lemonade for breakfast. It wasn't even worthwhile to get out of the sack and go to chow.

It was very much the same as when we were in Italy. We thought we had it tough there too until we began to see the tragic conditions under which Italians in the surrounding villages had to live. It was sad to drive through and see families huddled around a fire in an open barn or cave-like shelter. They had nothing. It was sadder still to see the young kids, holding cans, waiting next to our garbage cans to collect our leftovers.

When all of us nurses saw this, we started asking for extra food, keeping it as clean on our plates as we absolutely could so that we could put the food into the kids' pails instead of the garbage pit. The mess Sergeant came to us and told us that he knew what we were doing. He told us to take less food so that he could give the kids what was left after he had served mess. He said that it would taste better because it wouldn't have a trace of cigarette ash in it, and wouldn't be all messed up. Our doctors saw what we were doing and did the same. The enlisted men collected food from their mess and delivered it to the hungry people. We could only do this while we were a station hospital. There were no kids or family around when we functioned as an evacuation hospital.

Back at our location in Africa, we were also running short of all medical supplies. One of the most acute and distressing shortages, however, was the dwindling supply of toilet paper. All the paper had been removed from the patients' latrine, forcing them to come to us for it. We would then dole it out, three squares to a patient. Not only was there a lack of toilet tissue, but there was also absolutely no substitute we could use. Kleenex and newspaper were unobtainable. The poor guys would complain but we would remind them that 'war is hell' and present them with the inadequate three squares.

One morning the chief nurse called an emergency meeting outside our tents. She was in a rage. There was absolutely no toilet paper in the nurses' latrine. She informed us that someone had thrown our two allotted rolls down into the ditch. She also told us that this had incensed the old man so much that he refused to issue anymore to us. He screamed that since the nurses had caused the problem, then they could solve it as well.

The sad thing was there was no way to solve it. The only possible way would have been to 'borrow' some grape leaves from our neighbor, the farmer. That probably would not have worked either though, because I'm fairly sure none of us would have been able to distinguish grape leaves from poison ivy, and the end result would have been worse than no tissue at all. It was a terrible situation and everyone was screaming and yelling at once.

I shrieked louder than anyone, stating that whoever had done such a despicable thing should be hung by her thumbs. I no sooner got the words out of my mouth when one of my tent mates kicked me sharply in the shins and told me to "shut my big Irish mouth."

The Captain dismissed us with the threat that disciplinary action would be taken if the culprit were ever caught. When we got back to our tents I innocently asked why I had been so viciously kicked in my throbbing leg. Betty, one of my tent mates, asked me what I remembered about the previous night. Well, I told her, I did remember going up to the rec tent to write a letter. I could also recall getting into a discussion with a group of our doctors, but couldn't remember exactly how the discourse ended. In fact, I said, I couldn't remember getting back to my tent at all. The only thing I knew for sure was that I had slept very soundly.

With red faces and bulging eyes, my tent mates informed me that they had brought me home from the rec tent after breaking off my not-so-very intelligent conversation with my medical superiors. Before putting me in my sack they decided to stop off at the latrine. They insisted that they had only taken their eyes off me for an instant when I jumped up, grabbed the two rolls of toilet paper and threw them into the ditch, declaring that "I was sick of people watching how much paper I used."

They closed their narrative by agreeing with me that indeed the culprit, namely me, should be hung by her thumbs. I knew how angry everyone was, and knew that I never would have been able to laugh my way out of this one. I made them promise me that they would never tell anyone, and God bless them, they never did.

That was a frightening experience for me. I had never been drunk in my life. In fact, before joining the Army I never drank at all. I didn't believe that a person could drink and reach a condition where they could do something that terrible and not even remember that it had happened. While I was stationed at Ft. Monmouth, Major Newell had delivered many lectures on the evils of drink. She told us about nurses who had gotten pregnant and couldn't even remember who the father was.

I really thought at the time that it was just scary talk so that we wouldn't drink. I knew there were many things happening to me that I couldn't control, but getting ossified was not one of them. It actually was a good lesson for me because after that one time I never got drunk again. I would nurse a drink and the minute I felt a glow, would cease and desist.

This drinking thing brings to mind what happened to me one night in Italy. Some fly boys in an outfit near us sent over a truck to get any nurses who wanted some good food to eat. When we heard that magic word--food--about 15 of us piled into the truck. After I ate and the night progressed, I noticed that many bodies seemed to be falling by the wayside. I mentioned to an extremely young Captain that all his buddies appeared to be preoccupied with talk of sex and getting stinkoed.

Don't forget now, by this time I was a reformed drunkard who still had aspirations of entering a convent, come cessation of hostilities. We were standing at the bar and he told me about all the dangers they faced in aerial combat and that, who knew--"perhaps tomorrow we would all be dead."

I replied in all seriousness, "If I thought there was a chance I would be dead tomorrow, I would surely spend tonight on my knees (praying) and not on my back, satisfying your death wish."

He choked on his drink and rallied all his conscious buddies around to hear what I had said. I was mortified and, honest to hell, that phrase became as famous in Italy as MacArthur's "I shall return."

CHAPTER XI

When my brother, Harry, finally got the Mediterranean back under the control of the U.S. Navy, supplies started moving again. Medical supplies, food and mail started to arrive. I received a package from home that contained a beautiful pair of satin pajamas. Bunny, one of my tent mates who was also charge nurse in the operating room, came up with a wonderful idea. She went to the O.R. and got us a pail of hot water. I took a luxurious bath in a helmet of hot water, donned the satin pajamas and climbed into the sack.

I felt clean and feminine for the first time in months and proceeded to fall asleep immediately. I don't know how long I had been asleep when I awoke and felt something on my chest. We had always had field mice and lizards in the tent, but never before had they gotten so brave that one would nestle anywhere on my body. I got my hand out from under the covers to try to brush whatever it was away. I put my hand on my chest and damn near had heart failure. I felt an incredibly huge, bony, hairy claw-like hand, and even though I couldn't see any part of this monster, I knew he had to have a bolt in his neck.

I could hardly speak because my mouth was so dry. I finally blurted out, "What do you want?" as if I didn't know. "Don't be frightened. I know you and you know me," the hairy monster replied. When I heard his voice and thought I knew who it was, I became a little less frightened and concerned about being raped, but was still very upset. I reached for my flashlight, which was hanging on a C-Ration box next to my cot. Apparently my abrupt movement frightened him and he took off. I jumped from my cot and yelled for Bunny, who woke up and ran outside the tent with me. I started yelling for the guard, but everyone except the guard came running.

I told the old man that the guy had been outside my tent and had lifted the tent side to get to me. The old man had the gall to tell me that I had probably been dreaming and to go back to sleep. Bunny told him that before we had started our baths she had secured all the tent ropes and the ones on my side of the tent were undone, proving that someone had been there.

I was really in a bad state. I told the old man that I had been yelling for the guard and shining my flashlight at him but that he had completely ignored me. "Mickey," said my gallant C.O., with his arm around my shoulder in a loving, fatherly way, "that guard couldn't leave his post to come to you. He's guarding the dynamo, and while I love you dearly, I could replace you a damn sight sooner than I could get another dynamo."

Holy hell, I thought. Not only did the Army see me as an insignificant atom, but an expendable one at that. I realized that they were as contemptuous of me as I was of them. It surely wasn't a good feeling. One of my biggest complaints with the Army was how impersonal it was. Everyone was issued a number, and a number he remained until getting back into civvies. To the Army, Lieutenant G.I. O'Reilly was only an insignificant atom, but to Lieutenant O'Reilly, a pretty damn important one.

The adjutant hung around and asked a lot of questions. Did I feel an Army shirt attached to the hand or a patient's pajamas? I was no help at all. All I could remember was the giant, hairy hand.

Because I was so agitated, the chief nurse gave me a sleeping pill and I finally fell off to sleep. About an hour later my other two tent mates, who had been out on a date, returned and woke me up. They wanted to know all the gory details. They ticked me off by making light of the situation and for yelling at me because I didn't hold onto him for them to see.

After that, I really couldn't sleep. I popped another pill and was finally able to fall off, but then had to get up again at 6:00 and get dressed to go on duty. By that time I was feeling like a zombie. My poor corpsman saw the state I was in but didn't know quite how to handle my condition. In an effort to help me out, he signed my name to a pharmacy requisition that had to be in by 8:30 in order to be filled. The only reason he signed it was because he knew that I was unable to do so.

Needless to say, he caught hell for that Christian endeavor. When the pharmacist received the requisition he knew it was not my signature and, following procedure, contacted the chief nurse. She then returned with the corpsman to my ward. Once she saw the condition I was in, though, she understood why he had acted on my behalf. No disciplinary action was taken against either of us. She led me back to my tent where I fell on my cot and slept for the next 24 hours, awaking to go on duty the following morning at 7 a.m.

When I reported for duty the next day, a patient asked to speak to me alone. He asked if I knew who had come up the side of my tent the night before (by this time everyone in my tents knew the story). When I told him that I had an idea of who it was, he said he also thought he knew. Neither of us wanted to mention a specific name, so each of us wrote it down on a piece of paper and uncovered the letters one at a time. It was the same name.

I had suspected this specific person because he had been acting a little strange and kept following me around. My detective patient suspected him because he had awakened the previous night to go to the latrine and found the bed next to him empty. The missing man wasn't at the latrine and couldn't explain his absence. We decided to keep our secret. The poor guy was in for combat fatigue and I knew that he was going for counseling. I couldn't see any reason to add any more grief to the problems he already had.

The only laugh I got out of the whole situation was when I heard the scuttlebutt that made the rounds of the entire hospital. By then, the whole story had changed. My name wasn't even mentioned, and the rumor going around was that one of my tent mates (the laughing one) had been raped. Serves her right for laughing at my horrendous experience.

I know that I didn't wear those pink satin pajamas again for a long, long time.

CHAPTER XII

On five different occasions in my military life I had the misfortune of meeting five one-star Generals. Each encounter turned out to be a calamity. I never consciously said to myself, "Oh, a General--let's get involved." It just happened.

For many reasons, I will refer to all five by number only. My first experience, with General #1, was quite traumatic and one that I will never forget.

I was sitting in my tent in Africa, reading a book and minding my own business, when Jim Clemens, a Captain from the M.P.s, came in. He was extremely upset. He told me he had an eight-hour pass and wanted to spend it with Marty, our assistant chief nurse. He discovered that Marty had left the area and was out on a picnic with the chief nurse, a one-star General and the General's aide. He asked whether I would help him out. Being merely a Captain, he felt he couldn't possibly approach her, and asked whether I would intercede for him. Jim must have figured that, being a 2nd Lieutenant, I had nothing to lose. Not giving a thought as to what the consequences might be, I said O.K. and jumped in his jeep.

After driving a couple of miles we arrived at the site of the one-star picnic. What a sight--four nuts of high rank sitting in an African field in the middle of absolutely nowhere in about 95 degree weather, with the bright sun melting their heads. I walked up to the group, called Marty aside and explained the situation. She was all excited and wanted to go with Jim, but said she could only leave if I would take her place at the party. She must have seen the negative look in my eyes, because she quickly added that the General had brought some excellent food, they had a radio with good music and that the General's aide was quite good looking.

It was the food that made me say yes. Marty left with Jim and I joined the party, really the uninvited guest. The food was good, the chief nurse was pleasant, the General was a good sport for such an old guy and the aide was really young and cute. We ate, laughed and had a good time. When it was time to leave, we cleaned up the area and piled into the General's command car, with the General and the chief nurse in the back, and Junior and me in the front.

We had only driven a little way when I noticed that the General and Junior seemed to be getting upset. They were communicating in military terms with which I was unfamiliar. I didn't know what was wrong, but got the distinct impression that it was panic time. The General screamed, "Stop the car!" and Junior put 160 pounds of pressure on the brake. We stopped fast. Thinking it was a mechanical problem, I immediately jumped out of the car and, in order to keep things light, turned to the General and said with a big smile, "Don't worry, General--the A.N.C. will get you out of this situation!"

With eyes popping, he screamed at me to get the hell back in the goddamn car. It was at that moment I realized we were in the middle of a live minefield. It was with fear and not embarrassment that I became mute. I meekly climbed back in and never said another word as Junior backed up the car and maneuvered us to safety. When we got back to camp, I nodded goodbye and beat a hasty retreat to my tent.

If there had been a place to hide I would have found it, but there was no place to go. Besides, I knew that the chief nurse would have hunted me down no matter where I went.

She found me and berated me for acting like a child and for jumping out of the car with no fear for my safety. It seems that I was the only one who didn't know it was a minefield.

I was still mute and couldn't explain to her that my actions stemmed from ignorance rather than bravery on my part. She seemed particularly upset because I had told the General that the A.N.C. 'would take care of him.' "Did you know", she screamed, "that he was a General with the Tank Corps?"

I'm glad I was unable to speak, and could not say what I was really thinking. It seemed obvious to me that, given his background, the General should have known better than anyone that we were in the middle of a minefield.

Anyway, she was genuinely upset for about a week and I never got invited to go out with her again. She told the old man about it, and I heard that he thought it was funny until my affliction with Generals happened to a General buddy of his. But that's a whole other story, best left for another time…

Looking back on that fiasco, though, I have no regrets about what I went through that day because my help turned out to be the beginning of a wonderful thing for both Marty and Jim, and I was happy to be part of it. By the time I had interceded on his behalf I knew him well, but our relationship didn't exactly start out that way. I actually met him under rather embarrassing circumstances.

Anytime I was off duty and the enlisted men were going to play a baseball game, I had permission to jump into a truck and ride along with them. We had a 1st Lieutenant Administrative officer who had played great baseball for U.C.L.A., but since this was an enlisted men's ball team, he had to change his rank to Sergeant in order to play.

One day I went to see the enlisted men play the M.P.s. There was one enlisted man who looked a little older and heavier than the rest. I had a wonderful time razzing him all day. He was kind of slow when running the bases and I would yell at him to come over and get a vitamin shot. Every time he came to bat I would think of a smart-ass thing to say. Later that night, long after we returned to camp, I ambled into the rec tent and Marty called me over to her table. She said she wanted me to meet someone.

She introduced this big, good-looking Captain from the M.P.s. I shook hands with him and asked if he had seen the game. He replied that he had not only seen it, but he had also been aggravated as all hell by some female voice screaming at him from the sidelines. I almost died when I realized that he was the 'Sergeant' that I had been harassing all afternoon. He said he realized that I didn't know he was an officer but said that his men had gotten a big charge every time I called him a slow, old, fat man. He said he hated coming up to bat and thought that his men were clapping and rooting for the 74th.

I told him that I thought the biggest offense was not mine, but the fact that a military policeman, a Captain to boot, had lied about his rank and tried to pass himself off as a Sergeant. He laughed and said that all enlisted men's rosters were padded with a couple of old, large Sergeants who were officers in disguise.

We became good friends, so when he came to my tent looking for Marty that day I was happy to help him out. I was even happier when I learned that they had gotten married after their return to the states.

CHAPTER XIII

About two months after we set up in Mateur, eight of us--four doctors and four nurses--were given a 12-hour pass, the use of an ambulance, and permission to go into Tunis. We were almost as excited as if they had told us we were going home. We changed from our fatigues into Class A uniforms and headed for civilization.

We rode in the back of an ambulance and sang all the way. The doctors said they felt like they were out on a Sunday drive with their children, but we didn't care. We were happy to get away from camp and away from the war, even if only for 12 hours. How wonderful it was to see buildings again instead of tents, and to see all the Frenchmen in civilian clothes. It sure beat looking at Arabs in sheets.

The first thing we did was to find a restaurant, as far from a G.I. mess as we could get, even though we were warned not to eat native food. The biggest treat was that we would be able to sit at a small table with real chairs, china dishes and a white tablecloth. I got so homesick I almost couldn't eat.

It was the first time we had been out of camp with the doctors. This was a social occasion and I planned to make the most of it. Major Mack, one of the doctors, had a great sense of humor. I asked him to cut my meat as I tucked the napkin under my chin and proceeded to eat peas with my knife. He laughed and said he wasn't surprised at my eating habits because he knew I was from Brooklyn and figured that's how everybody who lived there ate. He didn't laugh, though, when I started sticking the leftover rolls into my pockets to bring back to camp. He knew I was dead serious about it and said it was embarrassing him. I thought to myself that I would rather be embarrassed than be hungry, but put the rolls back in the basket. I figured it was only fair to concede a point now and then, and to let it go. After all, I thought, Major Mack had been a good sport about the peas, so why not make him happy.

After we finished a good meal (expensive--it was Dutch Treat), we four nurses decided to lose the doctors. They were really starting to act like our fathers by then, and had even begun making out a schedule for the rest of the day without consulting us. I kept waiting for Major Mack to tell me to "sit up straight." We told the boys we would meet them at the Red Cross Club at 5:00 p.m. and took off on our own.

We went looking for someplace to buy souvenirs. We only went to seedy-looking places or street stands because we didn't have much money. I think every G.I. on leave in North Africa that day had the same idea, and that's what got us into trouble.

They say that women with maternal instincts become nurses and it must be true, because we surely had our protective antenna out. Every time we saw a G.I. buying some monstrosity like a velvet pillowcase with *"MOTHER"*, *"WIFE"* or *"SWEETHEART"* painted in scarlet, we would take it out of his hands and steer him towards something less flamboyant and less expensive. We explained that the cheaper pin or ring would probably be more to their loved one's fancy. We also talked the guys into doing a little more bargaining before settling on a price. This made us very popular with the G.I.s, but did nothing to enhance us with the marketeers.

We had so many Frenchmen yelling and creating a disturbance that the M.P.s finally came over to investigate the commotion. They advised us to move on, so we decided we had done enough good deeds for the day and moved on to sightseeing.

We visited a beautiful Cathedral and walked through some gorgeous flower gardens, but my day was made when I saw a woman holding a beautiful infant.

It took surprisingly little time to convey to her my desire to hold the baby. I couldn't speak French and she couldn't speak English, but she seemed to instinctively know what I wanted and smiled as she handed me the baby. What a feeling. I had forgotten how soft and cuddly and good smelling babies were. I had some horrifying thoughts about this WWII turning into another 100 Year War. I wondered how long it would be before I would get the chance to hold another baby. I handed the little one back to her with a tear and a thank you. I walked away and was feeling a bit depressed about this until I saw a sight I absolutely could not believe--a real authentic North African Public Men's Toilet.

It was one of the weirdest sights I had ever seen--a semi-circular metal barrier about 180 degrees in circumference and about four feet in height. The men would get behind it and urinate--wild! As I was approaching I could see the man's head and feet. As I walked past and looked (impossible for me to resist), I could see their backs. There was absolutely no mystery as to what was going on. I couldn't understand why the builders hadn't made it in a complete circle, with a door. I had to admit something I thought I never would--Army latrines were a one hundred percent improvement. I just hoped that none of the U.S. Army Engineers would ever see this setup and get any bright ideas. I didn't know what accommodations they had for females in Tunis and never asked. I really didn't want to know.

We finally made our way back to the Red Cross Club and picked up the boys. The ride back to camp was quieter than the ride out. I think the doctors were glad that we separated. They couldn't believe the stories we told. They must have enjoyed our company, though, since they took us out again when we got to Italy and visited Pompeii.

CHAPTER XIV

I can't remember the exact date we left for Italy, but it was probably around November 25, 1943. It was definitely the day before Thanksgiving. The word went out that we were going to set up an evacuation hospital there. We had to transfer all of our patients out, dismantle the tents, pack up our bedrolls and get the hospital packed on trucks.

Speaking of bedrolls, a very few, more fortunate and knowledgeable than the rest of us had a sleeping bag inside of their bedrolls. I don't know where they obtained them, but I do know they were not issued--for sure not to me. But I know from speaking to my husband Jim that the engineers would often 'swap' various and sundry 'articles' with the Navy and had a big advantage over the rest of us.

The Colonel announced that we would celebrate Thanksgiving a day early because the next day we would be in transit. The stoves were set up and we had our holiday dinner from mess kits. It was an outstanding meal with all the trimmings--turkey, potatoes, vegetables, gravy and pie--a real stateside Thanksgiving menu, that we ate sitting on the ground or on crates or the running board of trucks. But we were all together, and it was a beautiful meal.

After we ate we all headed for Bizerte, the port of embarkation. We emptied out of trucks and boarded a Navy ship, which looked something like a transport. After a time, we lifted anchor and sailed for Italy. The only thing I can remember during that trip was that we were all very cold and hungry. We were huddled together on the deck like a flock of sheep.

When we were about a mile from land, we were told to prepare for disembarkation. Thank God we didn't have to go the usual way--down nets attached to the side of the ship. Instead we were able to use a ladder which hung from the rail of the boat. Even though it was going up and down and sideways with the movement of the boat, it was more stable than the nets would have been. We all huddled on the deck, and when the bow of the ship opened, we marched into the water and onto the beach at Salerno. I don't recall the date we landed, and since we were not able to disclose this type of information to our family and friends, I never did record the details. All I remember is that we arrived about two months after the infantry and set up the evacuation hospital. Then we followed the 5th Army up the boot.

CHAPTER XV

The patients were always close to my heart. I was amazed and shocked at the ages of the infantrymen. They were 17, 18, 19, with an occasional 20-year old thrown in. One night I was in the rec tent writing home: "...Last night when I made rounds I tucked my angels into their mosquito netting. They look just like a lot of little babies when they are asleep with their yellow and brown and black hair mussed up on the pillow. They certainly don't look like the tough fighting men the Germans and I know them to be. I often think of the hundreds of mothers who would give anything they possessed to be in my place. It is a very comforting thought, especially when you get so fed up with everything that you want to throw in the towel..."

As I was writing, Captain Gold, one of our officers, came up to me. He said he had to leave for about 15 minutes and was expecting a British Army Major to come visit. He asked me whether I would buy the Major a drink and sit with him until he got back. "Sure," goody me said, so he gave me his bar card.

About 25 minutes later, he returned and asked whether the Major had come yet.

"Yes," I said. "He came and then left in kind of a huff."

"In a huff?" asked the Captain?

"Well, he started it," I said.

"Started what?" asked the Captain. "All I asked you to do was get the poor guy a drink."

"Well, I got him his drink," I said, "and he immediately started that old argument about how our boys always move in on the British women and take advantage of them while their men are away. He also threw in that old crap that Americans were also over paid, over sexed and over here. That really ticked me, Captain. I love the kids I take care of. I just mentioned to him that the British women weren't exactly hit over the head and dragged away, and that they seemed to enjoy the Yanks' company anyway--the same Yanks, incidentally, who were also putting their lives on the line to help you, Major, in your war. So, he finished his drink, grabbed his cap and left--like I said, in a huff."

The Captain stomped over to the next table where a group of doctors were playing cards. "Did you hear that?" he screamed. They all laughed and said, "Better still, we watched it. You're the jerk who asked an Irishman to buy a drink and to entertain a Limey. You're a Jew – you should understand and know that stuff."

As I was finishing up the letter I had been writing, Captain Gold came back and apologized to me for being so angry. He never knew that even if he had stayed away, I wouldn't have cared, because I defended my lads to an angry Brit Major and won the argument.

It was around this time that I encountered General #2. There was no entertainment in camp so the off-duty hours really dragged. To amuse ourselves, Mary, Oggie and I had made up a little trio. We didn't sound anything at all like the Andrew Sisters, but we were loud, and everyone could recognize the tunes. Mostly we made up parodies that amused the rest of the group.

One night the old man was in the rec tent, entertaining an old buddy who was a one-star General. He called Oggie and Mary over and asked them to sing a couple of songs. They had absolutely no desire to sing for a General. To get out of it, they told him they couldn't possibly do it without me and that I was on night duty. Not to be deterred, the old man sent Oggie to the tents where I was working to tell me that I should get relief for about half an hour so that we could sing for them.

Oggie went back and told the C.O. that I said I was sorry, but that I was very busy and could not, in all good conscience, get relief. Marty, who was there, said that the General couldn't believe his ears. He asked the old man what kind of an outfit he was running where a 2nd Lieutenant could refuse a request that was almost a direct order with, "I'm sorry, I can't come."

The Colonel said, "Oh, Mick never said that. Oggie, what did Mick really say?" Oggie, sort of flustered, started to hem and haw. "Really, Oggie," the old man said, "off the record, no fear--what did Mickey really say?" Oggie truthfully, but with a lack of some reasoning said, "Mickey says she's really busy doing some honest to God nursing and can't leave, but if you really want to be entertained, to get yourself a U.S.O. girl."

The old man turned to the General and said, "That's more like what the Mick would say." This was incomprehensible to the General, who told the old man he wanted to meet me when I got off, which would be in two days. Oggie came back and asked whether that would be O.K. with me. I couldn't believe my buddy actually told the old man what I had said, so to get out of the situation I agreed. I would meet the General.

The more I thought about it, the more frightened I became. There was no way I wanted to have a date with a General. When the memorable day arrived, I got myself completely lost. I went from tent to tent, playing hide and seek with everyone who was sent to find me.

The General came and left, and when I thought it was safe, I finally made an appearance. I was immediately sent to the old man's tent. I never saw him so angry. He said I had made a fool of him in front of his friend, and asked what in hell I was afraid of.

I don't know why I was so terrified, but a General was surely out of my league. The Colonel was upset, but he could see that I was more disturbed than he was. I apologized profusely. He knew how much I respected him. He also knew I was aware of a lot of mischief he let me get away with.

For instance, one time he was reading me the riot act for something I had done--I had made a flag out of a pillowcase--Girl Scouts of America Troop 74--and hung it outside my tent. He told me that despite the fact that I was one of the best nurses in the outfit, at times I acted like an airhead. I had replied, "Colonel, if I didn't laugh at some of the stuff that goes on here, I'd cry."

When I was apologizing for my latest conduct with his friend the General, I was very close to tears. He patted me on the head and said, "I know, Mick. If you don't laugh, you'll cry," and he forgave me.

He never mentioned the incident again, which endeared him to me more than ever.

CHAPTER XVI

My adventure in Pompeii was a trip I did not write home about. I wouldn't have known how to describe it to my folks.

The same group of doctors who had taken us to Tunis in North Africa took us with them when they went to Pompeii. Once again we went in an ambulance. I learned a lot of things that day. The first thing I discovered was how sick I could become while sitting sideways in a car and watching all the scenery receding into the background, like it was being swallowed up by a tunnel. The trip seemed endless.

We finally emptied out of the ambulance and discovered that we, except for a tour guide, were the only people there. I think the fact that it was early in the morning and also that Italy was at war had a lot to do with that.

We walked about, really enjoying all the sights--the petrified people and dogs, the rock-like loaf of bread in the bakery oven, the ruts made by the chariot wheels in the cobblestones--all fascinating sights to see.

The boys had hired a guide, and he didn't leave out a thing. He showed us the concrete phalli in the road that pointed the way to the whorehouse, and said that scientists always remarked on the color and brightness of the paint; paint that to this day can't be duplicated for its durability and lustrous brilliance. I had to agree with them. The paintings on the walls of the house of ill repute also looked as if they had been painted yesterday. They were all pictures of various sex positions, each life-like, painted over the stone couches beneath. They were impossible to miss. I kept my eyes on the ground because I was too embarrassed to look anyone in the eye. I had seen enough, had enjoyed the day and wanted to get back to the outfit and a nice, cool shower.

As we walked towards the ambulance we noticed that the doctors were involved in deep debate with the guide. We all gathered around to try to hear what we had been missing. We soon realized that the conversation was about the senoritas, which were us. Dr. Mack explained that all the boys wanted to see a picture that was under lock and key. The guide said he didn't want to show it to the women because he thought they might become offended. I couldn't believe that there could be anything more offensive than what we had already seen.

One of the females asked if the guide knew that we were nurses. I guess she figured that nurses have seen everything and could never be shocked or offended. I really didn't want to see any more, though, and said I would wait by the ambulance. I was told by everyone to "grow up" and to join the procession that was heading quietly toward the art display.

I had no idea of where we were--still in the ancient ruins, but off a little to the side. We approached this big column. About eight feet above us was a wooden plaque about three feet by three feet covered by a gray shutter, which was closed and secured with a large iron lock. The guide took a key from his pocket, opened the lock and pushed back the shutter. There was the picture. Painted in brilliant colors of red, black and gold, we saw an explicit picture of a man, holding the scales of justice. One tray of the scale was full of gold coins, the other with an enormous penis. The scale was balanced. I was never an art student, but I understood the meaning of that picture.

A couple of people said 'wow' but it was mostly quiet as we all walked back to our vehicle. Major Mack broke the silence by remarking that it was the first time he had ever seen me speechless. I replied, "Well, now, we all know why Mt. Vesuvius blew it's top."

The next day at camp, almost every corpsman approached me and said, "Mickey, Major Mack said you can tell us why Vesuvius erupted."

I have never, ever in my life met anyone who visited Pompeii and saw that painting!!!

CHAPTER XVII

There are very few things that I believe the Army did well, but one thing I can't praise enough is whatever method they used to choose men for the medical corps. The men in the 74th were terrific. They were great with the patients, knew when to push and exactly how far, when to be gentle and when not to be soft. I never saw a patient angry for any reason at a guy that was taking care of him.

They were also great to us nurses. I remember one night I was on duty and the patients were all asleep. It must have been around midnight and I had to go to the john. I told my corpsman that I was leaving to go to the latrine and asked him to cover for me. I had just settled on the darn thing with my long underwear at my feet when I heard artillery fire off in the distance. The noise seemed to be coming closer. I didn't mind dying as much as being found in my long johns so I started dressing fast. I ran out of the latrine into the arms of my corpsman who was coming to get me. I yelled at him for leaving the tent unattended and he said, "Mick, I'd feel bad losing you if something happened but I'll be damned if I'm going to let anyone find you in your skivvies." We both had a good laugh over that night.

Al was the corpsman on duty when I cried for the third time. I think the incident had more to do with frustration and anger than melancholy. One night I sent all the ambulatory patients to the mess tent for dinner. The food box came up for the bed patients who couldn't get to mess, but there were no utensils with the food. No knives, forks or spoons. I sent Al, my corpsman, out to round up some implements. He came back and said nobody had any. I couldn't leave the tent because I had a real sick kid, so I told him to go to the head dietician, who was running the mess, and to raise some hell. The food, which wasn't too good to start with, was now cold.

Al brought back some spoons. He also brought back Cookie, the nurse in charge of the mess. She was furious that I had sent Al down to create a disturbance. When I tried to explain that the guys couldn't eat without them, she stormed out of the tent yelling, "Let them use their fingers."

That really set the boys off. They began shouting, "Throw the shit out," "Put it on the floor and we will eat it like animals," "Send it to the damn Germans" and a lot of suggestions of where Cookie could put the food. Al gave out the spoons, but the guys were so mad, none of them would eat. I pleaded and apologized, but to no avail. I didn't cry on purpose, it just happened. I was ashamed that anyone could be so cruel to these great guys. I cried sincerely. They grabbed their spoons and dug in yelling, "Mickey, look--we're eating. We're eating." So the tears did some good.

CHAPTER XVIII

The fourth and last time I cried was the most memorable of all. It was such a bad experience that it has had a major impact on me to this day.

When the troops got bogged down at Monte Casino, we slowed down too. Our status changed from evacuation hospital to a station hospital. We were servicing a large replacement depot that had thousands of troops waiting to be assigned. Axis Sally came on the radio and warned that all the boys 'on the farm' were going to get it. The replacement depot was located on a dairy farm so we all knew what she meant. A couple of nights later the Germans did bomb, but missed the repo depo and hit a small Italian village in the hills.

I was on duty when they started bringing in all the civilian casualties--old men, young boys, women and children. This scene horrified me. I wasn't completely hardened to seeing the morbid sights of wounded men, and was still learning how to build up a resistance to the repugnance that surrounded us. It was almost impossible to deal with those feelings.

I think it was the sight of little limbs and the delicate faces of the small children that affected me the most. Men are expected to get maimed in war, not babies.

We did all we could to dress wounds and set fractures. I tried to comfort a woman who was crying hysterically. I discovered that she was concerned for her young daughter, who was missing.

I went from tent to tent looking for the child until I discovered the reason why she wasn't in the hospital. She was dead. I had found an old man who knew both the mother and the child and he told me what had happened. I brought him back and had to stand by helplessly as he told the mother this tragic news.

That had to be the worst day of the war for me. I hope I never forget that day in Italy. I'm sure I never will. It is one of the major reasons I became so actively involved in peace demonstrations later in my life.

CHAPTER XIX

I don't know why the grass always looks greener on the other side, but I do know that Army chow always tasted better when it was prepared and presented by someone other than a member of the 74th mess. Because of this, whenever an invitation to dine at any other mess was extended to us and a means of transportation was provided, we would never hesitate to jump on the other outfit's trucks to go to eat.

When we were functioning as an evacuation hospital, we never had the time or occasion to accept an invitation. We followed the 5th Army up the boot and when they moved, we moved. We ate C and K Rations just like the guys. When the troops were held up at Monte Casino, we also stopped. We were designated as a station hospital and were ordered to serve at the repo depo.

When we received the invitation to dine at the officers' mess at the repo depo, we accepted. The trucks arrived and we all jumped on and headed out. There were about ten of us, including our chief nurse, the same Captain and nemesis from my experience with General #1. Instinct told me not to be in her company at this social gathering, but once again, food was involved. It was no contest. Food won out.

The dinner tasted great, probably because it was warm and didn't bounce in the air when it was dropped on the floor. After dinner, we were all sitting in the rec tent, mellowing out on Italian red and chatting amicably, when the C.O. of the outfit came in. He was a tall, erect, very military looking man who was smoking a cigar as he entered. He definitely gave the impression of being the undisputed "Lord of the Manor."

He was also a one-star General, and the third one I encountered in my military career. I should have sensed the danger. All of the frolicking stopped as he cleared his throat--a signal that he was about to speak. We could almost hear all the muscles in the room tighten from the tension his appearance created.

He thanked us profusely for taking such good care of all the men under his command and ended by saying, "If I can do anything at all to help you in your treatment of my troops, will you let me know?"

Now--when most of the women my age were learning new vocabulary words, perhaps in college, I was learning the care and treatment of the human body. I had never learned about a rhetorical question--one that neither expects nor requires an answer. I learned about it that evening from my Captain when we got in the truck to take us back home to our outfit. She explained it to me with white-knuckle fists clenched together. I think that perhaps she had them clenched so she wouldn't hit me.

At the time I didn't realize that stupid questions should be ignored, so I raised my hand. When the surprised General nodded my way I said that I was in charge of the isolation tents and that we were having a real problem with scabies and impetigo. The General smiled, and from years of experience of passing the buck, he smoothly referred my question over to his sanitation officer to answer.

He pointed to a Major--a small squat man who, through clenched teeth, asked what the problem was. I told him that our tents were full of scabies and impetigo patients who, when we sent them back to the repo depo, returned to us in about a week reinfected.

"Lieutenant," he said, glaring at the brass bars I was wearing (an indication that I held the lowest possible rank in the Army Nurse Corps) "what is the census in your tents?" I meekly replied, "about 45." Speaking very slowly and distinctly, he said, "I wish to God I could tell you the census of my tents and some of my problems. I am permitted to do neither."

I was mortified. I think the reason I acted so insipidly was due to my frustration in having to spend so much time on the guys who had the scabies, giving me less time to spend on the sick men who needed real nursing care.

I caught hell in the truck. The Captain said I had been an embarrassment to her and had to realize that everything I did reflected on her--the good and the bad. She didn't mention any of the good things, and all of the bad things I had done popped into my head. I made a promise to myself that I would check a "free food" truck before hopping on one again, and if the Captain were there, then I would just go hungry.

However, there was a reason for the 'stupid' question that I had asked the Major at the General's request. About two weeks prior to the dinner at the repo depo, I had been involved in a disagreement with my ward officer, who was also the doctor in charge of my isolation tents. We had many patients from the repo depo suffering from scabies. Dr. Sam, the ward officer, was in the process of discharging one of the kids back to duty, which meant he would be transferred back to the replacement center.

When he was told, the kid innocently informed the doctor that he would probably be back again in a few days because the sanitary conditions at the depot were all screwed up. The Captain became angry at what he considered to be the patient's defiance and said that if he did return with scabies he would regret it.

Sure enough, about three days later he was readmitted to our isolation tents. The Captain was incensed. He called the Sergeant in charge of admissions and told him he was to pick up this patient every morning at 6:15 for an assignment. His task would be to clean out some sort of garbage or 'fat trap' right outside the patients' mess tent, a nasty job and in a location where everyone could see him.

The following morning when I was going to breakfast I saw my patient in hospital pajamas cleaning the traps. He was surrounded by patients and enlisted men who were laughing and heckling him. I went on duty and told Captain Sam that I thought it was a travesty of justice to humiliate the sick boy in that way. He told me that he was running the ward and that I should just do as I was told. I fumed all day.

The next morning I skipped breakfast and got to my station before the Sergeant came in to pick up the boy. When he arrived, I refused to release the kid to him and told the patient to stay in bed. The Sergeant argued with me a minute or so--he knew how angry Captain Sam was going to be. So did I, but I was too far gone to care. For the very first and last time in my military career I barked those famous words to the Sergeant--'that's an order!'

The Sergeant left alone and returned 20 minutes later, with a very pissed-off Sam storming in ahead of him. He asked why I had countermanded his order, and I said it was because I thought the patient had an elevated temperature. He asked me if I used a thermometer to take the temp and I answered that I had just felt the patient's head and it seemed hot. Sam turned and walked out of the tent, yelling at me that I was in big trouble. All the patients were sitting up in their beds watching the performance, but no one was laughing. I think they all knew how much trouble I was in.

I went to the head nurse and discussed the situation with her. She said that she had also seen the kid in pajamas working at the mess tent and wondered what was going on. She told me to go back on duty and that she would go see the old man. About ten minutes later the adjutant, the commanding officer's aide, came in and began reading from a thick book. He asked me where Sam was and I answered, "talking to you about my court martial."

He laughed and said that according to army regulations I was in the clear because it was unlawful to give a patient any kind of duty when he was under medical care. He said he would leave the book on Sam's desk and told me to be sure to have him read it. I couldn't believe that he wanted me to tell Sam to read the book--the same Sam who was probably so mad by now that he might be inclined to fracture my skull with it at the mere suggestion of doing such a thing. The adjutant knew I was right, so he went looking for Sam.

I had fantasies all afternoon about how pleasant it would be when the good doctor came back and apologized to me. He returned to the ward about 4:00 that afternoon, smiling like nothing at all had happened. He said he was surprised that we had such a big fight because we always got along so well together.

No apology or explanation was given, and the incident was never discussed again.

I was involved in another situation that was an embarrassment to the chief nurse, although the old man thought it was funny. One of the officers had invited me to the repo depo to watch a baseball game and to have supper, which I gladly accepted. The game ended before mess call and in order to kill time he took me to see their medical setup. As we approached the dispensary, he opened the door with one hand and pushed me inside with the other. The sight that greeted me froze me in time and space.

I saw ten men standing in a straight line all with their trousers draped at their feet. They were holding their 'family jewels' for the Captain, a doctor who was examining same. This was an authentic *short arm inspection*. We nurses had all heard of this, but until now, none of us had ever witnessed one.

I think that they were also frozen in time and space as well, because no one in the room moved a muscle.

I thought quickly and pushed backwards to get myself out of the room. I didn't know any of these guys from Adam, so all I cared about was keeping this incident hidden from any member of the 74th station hospital. Needless to say, I skipped supper and went directly back to my outfit, where I stayed in my tent all night.

The next morning I went to breakfast, filled a tray with food and headed swiftly for an empty bench. I had just seated myself when the old man looked up and yelled, "Mickey, I heard that you held a short arm inspection at the repo depo yesterday."

We were sitting quite far apart, so everyone heard his remark. I looked quickly at the chief nurse and she seemed to be strangling on breakfast. All the doctors and nurses laughed like it was a big joke. I knew that all of the enlisted men who were dishing out the food couldn't wait to get back to their area to spread the news. I found out later that the doctor who made the inspection had called the old man immediately after I had left and half the hospital already knew. I was called to the chief nurse's office to explain. She wanted to know all the gory details.

I was a celebrity and all my fellow nurses wanted a description of exactly what I saw. I added a lot to juice up the real story and gave a vivid description of the procedure. This great gossip spread like a forest fire on a windy day. Everyone knew about it.

Every day I would go on duty, praying that I wouldn't admit a patient to my ward who would ask, "Do you remember me from the inspection?" This was a ho ho that I could have easily done without.

Thank God we moved away from the repo depo shortly after that incident.

CHAPTER XX

On October 29, 1944, we were given orders to break camp. We were going to move up the boot and rejoin the 5th Army as an evacuation hospital again. We pulled down the tents, rolled up the beds and packed the trucks, ready to go. At the same time, the old man was taken up in a plane to pick out a spot for our new location. After he returned and the maps were checked, it was discovered that the Germans were still holding the location that he had chosen. We all had a good laugh at the old man's expense-- apparently he was very good at checking terrain, but not very good distinguishing between Stars & Stripes and a Swastika. We stopped laughing, though, when we got word that we would be going on temporary duty to general hospitals.

We were divided into two groups. One group was assigned to go to Florence. The other, consisting of six doctors, 30 enlisted men, nine nurses and Mickey, were going to Livorno. I was miserable about being on detached service again, especially to a general hospital, organized in the deep south. I hated general hospitals and had trouble understanding southern accents, but the move turned out to be a blessing in disguise that would change my life.

When we arrived at the hospital at Livorno we were delighted at the scene of splendor that greeted us. I think it had once been an old school. There was a real building and real beds, and not a tent in sight. The landscape was beautiful and it didn't look anything like a war zone. We couldn't believe our good fortune until our bubble was burst.

I don't know what was done to accommodate the guys or where the doctors were billeted, but we ten nurses were set up in the basement of the building. Our cots were set up in a corridor, five on each side of a long running carpet which led to the nurses' showers and latrines (bathrooms, that is–no latrines for these dainty southern belles.) The walls were tiled and the passageway was wide, long and well lit. It was extremely well built, like the corridor of a large hotel.

There was a constant parade of semi-nude bodies running in and out of our 'bedrooms.' We spent all of our sleeping and free time there. All the nurses from the south laughed each morning and night when they went down the corridor to get to the toilets and showers. I used to sit on my cot and would yell at them, "You lost the war. You lost the war," (the Civil War). This was the worst insult I could have tossed at them, but they thought I was only fooling and laughed. None of them ever knew how lucky they were that we weren't combat troops. If I had a gun, I would have shot them.

It was the subject of more than one letter that I sent home: "...Oggie and Mary just came running off duty. They managed to get transportation to town. Neither of them could find their hats and were swearing like a couple of front-line soldiers. I almost got hysterical which made them even madder. What a pair. I finally got them dressed and they are gone and except for a steady stream of nurses who are taking showers and a steadier stream who appear to have diarrhea, the corridor (our room) is almost deserted. ...The chief nurse is a Major. She went to take a shower. I was all for locking her in, but Marty wouldn't let me. The parade started at 6 every morning. Half of the outfit went to the toilet while the other half took showers. We were all awake but good old Oggie sat up on her cot and yelled, Left, Right, Left, Right. Our gals are all taking it in good spirits. I must stop now--the kids are all getting ready for chow. Mom, Marty says I am a pest. Every time one of these girls go through I put on an act and they all think I'm a bit touched. We all get a big kick out of the sympathetic look they give me…"

The corridor became our new home and we longed for our old tents. When we protested, we were told it was only a temporary arrangement and to stop bitching. It lasted until I left for home.

By the way, I never heard the word "complain" in my entire Army career. I saw it on paper, like on charts . . . "the patient's chief complaint. . . " but I never heard the word. It was always "bitching." Everybody said it. Everybody knew what it meant. After a few weeks it became as commonplace a word as any I would ever use in my vocabulary. I wasn't even aware that I was using the expression.

When I finally returned home we had a large, festive, family welcome home party. My brother Bunny started complaining about something and I said, without thinking, "Oh, Bun, quit your bitching. It's not that bad." My poor father almost had a stroke. His eyes rolled and he shook his head sadly. I felt terrible and admitted I had picked up some bad language. "Yes, indeed," he agreed, "Yes, indeed."

That moment in time came back to me again a couple of months ago when I was told about an Army nurse who was home after serving in Vietnam. She was also at a festive family gathering, and asked her father to "Please pass the f___ing potatoes." I had to laugh. Same Army, different war. I know how she must have felt...

Back at the hospital we got busy, so tents were set up in the courtyards and gardens to handle the overflow of patients. Guess who they picked to staff the tents? Yes, the Yankee nurses who were on--not detached service--but servitude (slave) service to them.

Once we settled in, I had to go on night duty and guess where I went? Tent City! I loved it because it got me back to the casualties, but it was very busy. I wore fatigues and filled every pocket with medication--pain pills, cough medicine, bandages, dressings, adhesive tape, rubbing alcohol and eight-inch scissors, which I hung from my belt loop. I was a walking drug store.

In all this confusion, a 1st Lieutenant came in and told me that a General from the 10th Mountain Division was coming in to visit his soldiers who were in my tents. She then asked if I knew how to address a General when he made rounds. "Sure," I said, "Hi, General!" but she didn't laugh. She told me I would need to go to the tent entrance, stand at attention, salute him and give him my name and rank. I would then take him to each patient from his Division. She also told the guys from the 10th who were ambulatory to stand at attention when he entered the tent.

I told all the guys to be good boys, explaining the trouble I had already had with Generals. I told the fellows from the 10th to give me a sign if they were one of the General's boys and begged again for their cooperation. I also told one of the ward men to let me know when the General arrived and then continued with my ward duties.

The corpsman yelled "Mick," and I ran to the entrance of the tent, where this stranger was standing there looking at me. I stood at attention, threw him my best salute, and said "General, Sir. Lieutenant O'Reilly. May I take you to your troops?"

He looked at me and seemed puzzled for a moment, like he didn't know what the hell to do. He put his hand to his helmet, tipped it and said, "How do you do, Ma'am." My eyes almost popped out. He smiled at me and then pointed to the scissors that were hanging like a sword at my side. He said he didn't think that medics were supposed to carry arms. I agreed with him, and said I only wore it in case it was ever necessary to kill myself, like if I ever got into a situation just like this one.

He laughed. I laughed. The guys almost died. They had all been holding their breath until the General laughed and set us free. We made rounds--the General, his aide, the 1st Lieutenant night supervisor and me. When he left he shook my hand and told me I had been so military that he hadn't known what in hell to do. I had been the only nurse he had to meet. We said goodbye and I went back to my duties. A rather peaceful end to my encounter with General #4.

I went to mess at about midnight and asked if anyone else had met the General. One angel of mercy said that when he came in the front of the tent, she ran out the back, and didn't have to meet him. He didn't have any other men in the rest of the hospital.

His Division was the 10th Mountain Division. They had just arrived from the states and were set up in a staging area where one of the fellows walked into a minefield. When his buddies saw that he was in trouble, they ran en masse to help him. There were many casualties. That's the way they were. They instantly ran to help their buddies and never thought about the dangers. How could you not love and respect them.

CHAPTER XXI

The only good thing about being in this location was that the outfit had a Catholic chaplain, and that meant Mass every night--some spiritual food for which I was starving. The chaplain was Father Farrell, a wonderful Irishman who had great compassion and a terrific sense of humor. The kids loved him, but all of us knew he would never tolerate any disrespect. I called him Pop, and we got along great.

He told me a story one time about his dad that was typical of the Irish. I loved it. He said that in his parish stateside he was a chaplain in the county jail. His brother, who was also a priest, was chaplain in the poorhouse of another parish. His father, like most Irish parents, was proud as all hell of his two boys. The old man was boasting one night about the two wonderful sons he had sired when some old sop said to him, "How good are they– one ended up in jail and the other in the poorhouse." He said the patrons of the bar had to climb on the old man's back to keep him from beating up his Irish buddy...

Pop told me about the great discussion group he held every Tuesday night, and talked me into attending the meetings. I thought the first one was a disaster. There were about 30 guys there and no nurses. It reminded me of my high school catechism class with a nun in charge. Apparently Pop could see how bored I was and asked what changes I would make. I could tell by the gleam in his eye that he considered me a 'little miss know-it-all,' so I gave it to him straight. I said I would want to see discussions of some more important subjects, like whether the Vatican should be trimmed with gold plate while people outside were starving. We did that topic the following week and the meetings from that point on became much more exciting. They even included a little yelling.

For instance, one of my patients had picked up a ball and a couple of gloves at the Red Cross one day and wanted to have a catch. He asked another patient if he would like to play and the kid said no, that his religion forbid him to play ball on Sundays. The first kid, who I knew was Catholic because I had seen him at Mass and at the discussion group, replied that it was one of the stupidest things he had ever heard.

"Whoa," said Mom Mickey. I asked him whether he ate meat on Fridays. He said no, that he was not allowed to. I then said, trying to make a point, that I thought that was a lot more stupid than not playing ball on Sundays. The kid gave me a death look and ran as fast as he could to Father Farrell to report me and to add this topic to the agenda for the next Tuesday night discussion group.

At the next meeting, we discussed the concept of respecting beliefs that were different from our own. All was going well until one kid said, "Do you think Jesus played ball on Sundays?" I couldn't resist this opening and commented, "I'm sure He didn't because that law was made up by His Father and He had to obey His Father." That led to a discussion about the differences between the Old and New Testaments and it lasted a couple of weeks. I had no problem with the laws of the Commandments but church laws gave me as much trouble as Army laws. These discussions were good. It gave me a great opportunity to sound off about the differences between God's laws and church laws.

When we were at Cassino we had some German prisoners under our care. One day a young patient asked me if I had any problem with the idea of taking care of a Kraut. I said no, a patient is a patient and I would do my best on him. He left and came back a few minutes later with another question. He asked me how I would react if two patients came in on a truck and one was a German and the other was my brother. Which one would I do first?

Well, I told him I would check them and if they were both in the same physical shape I would do my brother first, but if the German were in worse shape and in more serious condition, I would do him first. The poor kid walked away shaking his head.

While I was censoring the mail that night (a job left to night nurses) I picked up a letter he had written home to his mother. He told her how much I had disappointed him. "I'm trying to kill them and she's trying to save them," he wrote. That letter left me depressed for days.

CHAPTER XXII

When the troops were pushed back a little in Belgium I think it bothered Command in Italy, and things started to tighten up. During that time, the Colonel put together a plan on how we would proceed if it became necessary for us to evacuate. His main concern was how patients who might be too sick to move would be cared for in the event we had to leave.

He came and asked me if I could speak German. I told him I had studied it for two years in high school, but that was it. He said he had already seen that in my file and wanted to know whether I would be willing to stay with a doctor and whatever patients could not be moved. I immediately agreed and was very pleased when he told me the doctor would be Tom Schrier, a man I respected very much.

The old man left and came back accompanied by a corporal. He directed the both of us to have a conversation to determine whether I would be able to speak and understand it. We began our chat in German:

The Corporal started by saying, "Can you speak German?"

I replied, "Yes, I can speak German."

"How much?"

"Well," I said, "I studied German in school for two years. I can say good morning, mother, good morning, uncle--father, friend, brother, sister, grandfather, grandmother. I can say table, chair, desk, door, and window. I can say stand up, sit down, you are a mule, you are a donkey, I am a girl, you are a boy and you are crazy."

He said, "Say something important."

I wasn't exactly sure what the word he said meant, but knew that it had to be important. I also knew that this would be my final chance. All of a sudden I remembered a play we had done in school. My part was that of a woman with a child who goes on a train and sees a man smoking. My line, delivered in a very angry tone was, "Can't you see the sign on the door that says smoking is forbidden here?" I had this down pat because it was also the only line I had in the play.

I repeated it to the corporal with the same anger and feeling, and then took a quick look at the old man to see how I was doing. He was eating it up. It sounded like authentic German to him. I then said to the corporal in German that I was not afraid. I wanted to go, and that was all.

The old man asked the corporal how I did. The corporal asked whether anyone else spoke German. The Colonel told him no, that I was it. Well, then, the corporal said, he guessed I could. The old man was almost singing as he walked away.

The corporal turned to me laughing and said, "Mick, I got all that garbage about all your relatives and about all the animals I am. But what in hell was that bit about smoking?"

He said that when I said I wasn't afraid, he knew he would tell the Colonel that I was O.K. Thank God, though, I never had to stay.

Later on, I spoke to a classmate in nurses' training, Doris Hanlon, who was in a station hospital in Belgium.

She told me they had to pack up their patients and leave everything behind. She said that when they returned the only thing missing from all the tents were all the nurses' underwear and stockings. I guess the German boys had decided to look for some girls.

CHAPTER XXIII

I wonder if I could be called a latent anarchist. When I was young I loved everything and everybody. I wasn't aware of the injustices surrounding me. I had a strong faith and trust in God and that security included my church and my government. My country--right or wrong--and didn't Jesus found the Catholic Church by tending its care to Peter and the Disciples?

In my early years it took all my effort just to get through nurses' training. The hospital work and patient care was effortless and pleasant, but the book part was tedious and difficult. I was never a brain, so for three years I waited for the axe to fall. When I graduated and passed State Boards, I couldn't believe my good fortune. As soon as possible I donned my Army uniform and went off to war.

I thought it was a just war. Hitler was an evil man and he had to be stopped. I was 21 years old and for the first time my eyes were opened to injustices.

Army regulations have always bothered me. I think the rules are too rigid. Do this but don't do that, even when doing what you were not permitted to do would be the right way to go.

A perfect example of this would be the day I observed a Sergeant with a squad of men who were building a shower while we were dismantling the hospital to move to Italy. I asked him if he knew we were moving, and he said it didn't matter to him because he had orders to build the shower. I asked him whether he would give the guys a smoke break until a superior officer came and changed his orders. He said no, and I walked away listening to the sounds of the hammer banging to the tempo of 'never disobey a direct command,' wondering how we could possibly win this stupid war.

In reality the U.S.A. had just built a beautiful camel wash; for there was no one left to use the shower.

While still on detached service at a general hospital in Livorno, there was an incident that caused my unhappiness which probably would not have occurred in my own outfit. For the first time, the trivial feelings of annoyance for Army regulations I usually had became of major importance.

I was on duty when the chief nurse, a Major, called me to her office. She was visibly upset and I couldn't think of what I had done to cause her anger. She told me that a young enlisted man--a private, mind you--had come to her office looking for me. She then asked whether I was aware of the Army regulation stating that officers were not permitted to associate with, mingle with or date, enlisted personnel. I had no idea what she was talking about. She said she would give me exactly five minutes to speak with him, and that I was to explain that this must never happen again.

When I entered her office I saw a young boy who had been a patient of mine a few months before. He must have been all of 18. I had called him Junior and he had called me Mom. I hadn't seen him since he had been discharged back to duty.

I could see that he was very agitated and hyper and I knew immediately that this was not just a friendly visit. He apologized for coming. He said the Major had reamed him out and he was sure he had gotten me into trouble. When I reassured him and he calmed down, he told me why he had come. He said he was A.W.O.L. from his outfit because he was afraid he was going to be killed.

An Infantryman A.W.O.L. in a combat zone during wartime could be tried and executed regardless of age or circumstances. He didn't know what to do or who to talk to. He had been eating at the Red Cross and sleeping in the fields. He said he had met a buddy earlier that day who had been a patient with him in my outfit and found out that I had been assigned to temporary duty at this hospital.

I didn't know what to tell him because the problem was beyond my capabilities to solve. I thought the best thing would be for him to see a chaplain. I also stressed how important it would be for him to return voluntarily to his outfit. I knew that our allotted time was almost up, so I pleaded with him to meet me in Livorno at 7:00 that evening and that I would hitch a ride there as soon as I got off duty. I told him exactly where to wait.

When the Major opened the door and came in she could see that we had both been crying but she never even asked what was wrong. She ordered us not to see one another again, and Junior left.

I tried to explain to her that he was 18 and I was 24 and that we weren't in the middle of a torrid love affair. I didn't dare tell her what the problem really was, figuring that she would probably call the M.P.s and turn him in.

The minute I got off duty I went into Livorno and started looking for him. I walked around the town for about two hours, but to no avail. I returned to my bunk sick and shaking. I tried to think of what I could have said to him but I had no answers. All I could do was pray, so I prayed hard for both Junior and myself--Junior for courage and safety, myself for patience in dealing with Army regulations.

I know that it would be impossible to run and win a war without rules. I also know that soldiers can't be allowed to walk off the line. But I believe to this day that if I had been able to put Junior in touch with someone more knowledgeable in this area, they would have been able to help him solve his problem. I felt the Army had let Junior down as much as Junior had let down the Army.

Junior was a number, the finger my C.O. had talked about, who was there to pull a trigger. It was just like General Bradley had said. The Army would never acknowledge the body and soul of a young boy.

I thought about him a great deal during the months that followed. I never did find out whether he took my advice to go back, or whether the M.P.s had picked him up. I still don't know.

St. Paul says to gird yourself with the armor of faith. Gird your loins with truth, a breastplate with justice and feet shod with peace. This was probably the first real dent in my armor.

CHAPTER XXIV

We all settled down into living in the corridor. While off duty, we missed sleep and quiet because of the constant parade to the showers and toilets; while on duty, we were continuously fighting the civil war with all the rebels at the hospital. Then it was Christmas Eve.

I wanted to go to confession and receive the Eucharist at Midnight Mass. It wasn't a real confessional. Father Farrell just sat in a chair and the confessor knelt by his side. I noticed that the nurses were taking much longer to confess than the guys, and had amusing thoughts as to what antics might be causing them to keep kneeling for so long. Then it was my turn. I knelt, made a simple, sincere and boring confession, and then waited for my penance. I figured one Hail Mary. But the following took place:

Father: "Are you dating any married men?"

Mick (hesitantly, and surprised): "What do you mean by dating?"

Father: "Going with, associating with, spending time with."

Mick: "Well, there is an officer at the repo depo that picks me up and takes me to baseball games and sometimes to his mess to eat."

Father: "Why didn't you mention it?"

Mickey (getting slightly annoyed): "Because there was no sin. If you want, I could make one up. I sure wouldn't call it dating."

Father: "I think you are committing a sin of scandal."

Mickey: "That's ridiculous."

Father: "How would you feel if you were a wife at home and discovered your husband was taking a nurse out, for whatever reason?"

Mickey: "I drove with him to Florence once to help him pick out a tablecloth for his wife."

Father: "The fellows see you at Mass and at the discussion group, and then see you out with a married man. That's giving scandal."

Mickey: "I see nothing wrong in what I'm doing."

Father: "Well, I do and I'm the one giving the absolution. I'm making this one conditional. If you see him again that makes the absolution void. If you are having a problem trying to see my point of view, maybe you could bring the situation up at our next discussion group. God Bless!"

End of confession, start of contemplation.

I went to my cot, smoked a half pack of cigarettes and was finally able to admit to myself that deep down, I knew Father Farrell was right.

I was supposed to go to a party at the Red Cross Officer's Club with that guy on New Year's Eve. I wrote him a letter canceling the date and went looking for someone to deliver it to him. I can still remember how very sorry I felt for myself that night. Little did I realize at the time that it would turn out to be the best thing that ever could have happened to me, and one of the biggest blessings of my life.

CHAPTER XXV

While walking to Mass later that evening, I had many things to think about. It seemed like a great deal was going on, and that there were some key issues I would need to sort out. I always felt better when attending Mass though, and especially enjoyed going to Midnight Mass on Christmas Eve. The experience of that evening turned out to be just what I needed, and helped me put everything in perspective again. I went back to my tent feeling refreshed, and found myself thinking about what I would include in the letter that I would write home later that evening to my parents:

Christmas Night, 1944
Italy

Dear Mom and Dad,

This is the day, darlings, that I have been dreading for almost a month, but the good Christmas Babe wouldn't let anyone be unhappy on His birthday so today turned out to be a beautiful spiritual one for me. As I start this letter it is 9:10 Christmas night.

Last night at 11 o'clock Kelly and I took Mary (Dutch Reform) to Midnight Mass. It was one of the most beautiful services I have ever attended. There was a choir made up of nurses and personnel who sang the Mass in Latin. I was sorry that I couldn't be in it but I was on night duty when they practiced. A very famous Italian opera star sang the Ave Maria and we all sang Christmas carols.

The place was jammed, mostly with patients, and a small stage was decorated beautifully with a Christmas tree and a small crib. It was a Solemn Mass and I felt closer to you in spirit than I had ever been since I left home.

The thrill of the evening came when 25 German prisoners sang Holy Night in German. It seemed so strange to hear these supposed enemies of ours, singing a hymn in praise of our God. I looked around at the faces of the patients. Boys with arms and legs in plaster casts, with patches on their eyes and some leaning on crutches, but I could not see any hate or bitterness in their eyes. In fact, through the tears in my eyes I could see the tears in theirs.

When I went up to receive Holy Communion I felt closer to God than ever before, and for the first time in my life I knew what was meant by "Peace on earth to men of good will," because peace certainly reigned in our hearts and these sick and sorely wounded boys certainly showed love and forgiveness to each other and proved their good will. It was wonderful and what a beautiful present the Little Babe in the crib received when almost the entire congregation received His Body.

Today was a typical Christmas day. It was freezing outside and I had 60 little soldier boys who kept yelling for Santa. Kitty, the nurse I work with, and I decided that something drastic had to be done and that it was up to us to do it. I went over to my barracks bag and gathered up my 2 bottles of whiskey (a 2-month ration). I kept looking around and my eyes kept coming back to the fruit cakes my family and friends had sent to me. I had seven cakes left so I added 6 to the whiskey and rushed back to the ward.

The doctor, Captain LoRe who also comes from Brooklyn and is a member of the 74th, brought out some more cake and candy to add to the feast. We sent to the Mess Hall and got 15 cans of evaporated milk, and some powdered eggs and guess what we made? Righto--old-fashioned Christmas Eggnog. Then we stacked up all the boxes the Red Cross had sent to us to give to each patient and 60 packs of cigarettes and started our party. It was a wonderful success. You could just about taste the whiskey in the eggnog. Imagine 2 bottles for 60 men but the boys really loved it.

Then Kitty and I sang for them. They in turn entertained us--Hillbillies, moonshiners and Texas cowboys all sang native songs for us and we had a wonderful time. It could not have been better if we had planned it for weeks. They are so wonderful, and so grateful, and I enjoyed it just as much, or even more than they did.

So tonight, on looking it all over, I realize that in a very strange way, this has been one of my happiest Christmases. But oh, how I wish now that I were home with you. I think that I would have been happy today even if I had been shut up in a room all by myself, because you both gave us kids so many happy and loveable memories to carry through life with us.

It's time for bed now and my Christmas Prayer will be in thanksgiving to God for giving me such wonderful parents--and a prayer that He will keep you safe for us for many years to come. Good night and God bless you darlings.

    Sis

CHAPTER XXVI

It would be very romantic if I could say that the first time I saw Jim Allen our eyes locked, my heart thumped, bells rang and I heard heavenly music. The truth of the matter is that I saw first saw Jim while we were attending a New Year's Eve party, and he was dancing with a 1st Lieutenant. I watched him laughing, dancing and having lots of fun while I was sitting next to a moronic 2nd Lieutenant who couldn't dance, wouldn't smile and looked like he was yearning to be somewhere stateside.

I had a miserable time New Year's Eve and decided that I would stay at home in my busy corridor reading books and writing letters. After about two weeks, though, I finally agreed to go out on a blind date with an officer from the Engineering Corps that a friend had lined up. The date was January 13, and I was happy to discover that the blind date was the same guy I had been wishing I had been with on New Year's Eve--the laughing, dancing one. We went out as a foursome to the Red Cross Club in Livorno and had a good time. I found out he came from Connecticut and had spent six years in the seminary before leaving there to join the Army.

The first dance really did it for me. I wasn't looking forward to getting up and dancing. I would have preferred to sit and talk, but the moment came when he said, "Let's dance" and we got up. When I was finally in his arms and he put his cheek on my face, I nearly fainted.

I asked him what kind of powder he used as an aftershave and he said Johnson & Johnson's baby talc. He said his skin was very sensitive and that his Mom had sent the powder to him from home. I said I knew it was Johnson & Johnson baby talc because his face smelled like a 'newborn baby's behind.' It reminded me of the nursery in the

Norwegian Hospital, and I told him it was making me homesick. The minute I said it I could feel his body tensing up and figured that my big mouth had blown it once again for me. But he laughed and I laughed and we both relaxed and bonded. We both had a good time and made another date to go out--this time alone.

The second date he came to pick me up in an Army jeep--no cost, free gas. We went to see an Army movie--a freebee, no cost. After the movie we went to the Red Cross and drank free coffee. The only cost for the entire night was ten cents for the two doughnuts. He was really embarrassed when he had to ask me for the dime. I didn't have a cent to give him either, because I also had no money. We were in a war zone and there was no place to spend money, therefore no one carried any. Money was used exclusively for playing cards. I never let Jim forget that first date. I told him I only married him because I thought he had wads of money stuffed in his combat boots.

CHAPTER XXVII

Four months into what was supposed to be our 'temporary' assignment at the general hospital in Livorno, I had another memorable run-in with the notorious Major. I was a mere 2nd Lieutenant working under a 1st Lieutenant who was in charge of a ward of amputees. I had finished all my assigned tasks about thirty minutes before mess was to be served. I asked the guys what the second best thing I could do for them would be if I could grant them a wish (I knew without asking what the first thing was.)

They all said the same thing--to get their heads washed. I got a few buckets of soap and water, and proceeded to carry out their wishes. They all had G.I. haircuts so it didn't take too long to wash each head. As I was getting ready to start the third one, the 1st Lieutenant called me away from the guys and told me not to do any more shampoos. I asked her if there was anything else she wanted me to do and she said to go get myself a cup of coffee. This didn't make any sense to me at all, and I wanted more of an explanation.

She said that what I was about to do just wasn't done. I still didn't understand until I looked over and noticed that the third head belonged to a young black boy.

"It surely can't be because he is black," I said.

"You don't understand these things because you are from the north and I am from the south" she replied.

"No, damn it," said the 2nd Lieutenant to the 1st Lieutenant, "it's because I'm a Christian and I don't know what the hell you are--not even humane."

She screamed, "That's an order," so like a good little Army nurse I slinked away to clean up my mess while she ran to report me to the Major. When she returned she called me to the phone and said the Major wanted to speak to me.

The Major told me to go off duty immediately and to return the following night at 7:00 p.m. for a shift of night duty. I had just finished a tour of nights and knew that this order had nothing to do with a need for night nurses. It was disciplinary action to show me who was in charge. I went off and did the two weeks. The good Major assigned me because she hoped it 'would teach me respect for rank.' The lesson didn't work. It just added to my confusion about how promotions were awarded.

How I wish now that I had taken a stand and had not been so weak or willing to comply. Army regulations state that an order given by a superior officer must be obeyed. The superior officer does not have to be moral or more intelligent. They simply have to be of higher rank. It would have been interesting to see what the outcome would have been had I been more gutsy. I wish I could relive those circumstances again. Had I taken that stand, I believe the moral issues which would have surfaced would have forced controversial questions to be addressed.

On a happier note, one night right after that incident I was working the tents, my corpsman came in and said that there was an officer outside looking for me. I went out and discovered it was Jim. I started yelling at him, reminding him that I was on duty and had no time for visits, in very much the same way Flo Nightingale would have done. He put his hand inside his coat and pulled out a pair of fleece-lined slippers. He told me he had seen them in the P.X. and got them because I had said my feet were cold. I was very, very impressed.

When I finally got off nights, we spent as much time together as we could. Most evenings we went to his outfit to spend time with his friends and have some good food. I felt no shame eating the cookies the girls from home had sent him. I even reminded him to send thank you notes so the cookies would keep coming. We didn't get to spend much time together, but whatever time we had was golden. We covered every topic. Sometimes we agreed, sometimes we had discussions, but he never raised his voice, which annoyed me a little bit because it kept me from raising mine.

About five years after these anxious days, Jim told me how impressed he was that I never laughed at dirty jokes anyone told me during the time we were dating. He said he didn't realize until after we were married that the reason I didn't laugh was because I didn't understand them. This was true. I was naïve to the point of stupidity.

I just enjoyed being with him. He was a lot of fun and very good company. I knew I could always relax around him, knowing that the night would never end with me struggling to defend my virtue. I felt safe and secure with him. We knew each other better than some couples did after going together for years.

CHAPTER XXVIII

In the middle of March I received a letter from home that my Dad had cancer. I knew that every month the chief nurse in Florence had been selecting the name of a nurse (drawn from a hat) who would then rotate back to the states on a 45-day leave. At the end of 45 days they would return to duty in Italy. Up to that point, three nurses had been home and back.

On our first day off, Jim drove me to Florence to see my boss about going home to see my father. My fingers were crossed all the way there. She understood my predicament and said that I would be the next to go, but first--and here's the catch--I would have to tear up the request I had made to be sent to an evacuation hospital. I had written the request when our status changed from an evacuation hospital back to a station hospital. I tore up my letter and then she added insult to injury by telling me she would also put me in for promotion to 1st Lieutenant.

I couldn't believe my ears. "Why a promotion now," I asked. "Well," she exclaimed, "I couldn't possibly give you a promotion while you're waiting to transfer out. That would mean you would be replaced by a 1st Lieutenant and that wouldn't be fair to the rest of the girls in the outfit." Her premise was that it would be unfair because it would not leave an opening for another nurse to receive a promotion. As far as I was concerned, it was simply the Army once again giving me a bite in the behind just to prove they could. I really didn't want the promotion.

The return trip Jim and I made from Florence to Livorno was a quiet one. I couldn't believe that I was volunteering to leave this guy who had become such an important part of my life. I had no idea how sick my father was, and wanted to be at his side, but I was also giving a lot of thought to the relationship that was developing with Jim. He was the first to bring up the subject when he said, "What about us?"

"I'll be back in 30 days," I replied quickly. He asked if I was planning to visit my mentor from high school, Sister Mary Louise. If I did, he also wanted to know what I was planning to tell her. I honestly didn't know what to say. She had written to me every month since I joined the Army and she knew me pretty well. Every day of doing Army time seemed to weaken my chances of ever surviving a religious life. Sister told me one time that I had some rough edges that would have to be smoothed out, but those edges had become more sharp and ragged. They were also more in number, and would have to be smoothed with a steel file.

Of the three vows of poverty, chastity and obedience confronting me, the only one I feared was obedience. The only reason I had entered nurses' training instead of the convent after graduation from high school was because I wanted to ensure my nursing vocation. But three years later I had still done nothing at all about controlling my mouth or working on my dignity. The fact that I was very opinionated was no secret. Everyone constantly mentioned it to me. There would be giant obstacles in my way to fulfilling my spiritual ambitions. If I had trouble with Army rules, what would I do with the convent ones? I concluded that I was probably not good convent material and just kept praying.

When I asked Jim about his feelings about the seminary, he said he left the seminary mostly because he wanted a family--a large family. He said that after the war he planned to start one, and that he hoped it would be with me.

The ball was in my court. We had been playing this mental game for ten weeks. In normal, peacetime, civilian life, after this length of time we would have been friends or acquaintances, but now he was waiting for a commitment. "Let's see what happens when I get back," I said, squirming my way out.

While waiting for the transfer to come through that would separate Jim and I and send me stateside, I had my final encounter with a General. Fortunately, it wasn't a very big deal because no one ever heard about him and I didn't get into any trouble. I was still on detached service and was working on a floor with about 50 beds. I knew there was a one-star General on the census but I had never seen him. He had a private room off to the side and didn't take any meals with us. He just kind of used the place like a hotel.

I had sent the ambulatory patients to mess and was serving chow to the bed patients when a smart, good looking 1st Lieutenant came up and said, "The General will have his dinner now." I couldn't believe that a one-star General would eat our humble chow, so I replied, "I have to feed the guys." Then the aide said in a crisp, in-charge voice, "This is General What's His Name." (I don't remember what.) Without stopping I replied, "I don't care if his name is General Eisenhower."

As the words left my mouth, my eyes looked down to the floor and I saw the shiniest brown oxfords I have ever seen in my life. Covering the oxfords was a pant leg with a crease that could cut through paper. I knew that the star would be there when I raised my eyes.

Sure enough there it was, sitting on the collar of a beautifully ironed shirt. I said a fast, "Please God, get me out of this" and He did. I looked the General straight in the eye and said, "I was told that the troops had to be fed before the officers, Sir." The General looked straight back at me and said, "That is true. I'll wait."

I have no idea where I had ever heard that statement about feeding the troops, but when I checked with the patients in the officer's ward, they said that it was true. I was convinced that God had put those words in my mouth. Oh, the power of prayer!

CHAPTER XXIX

Almost all of the bad things that happened to me during my Army career occurred while I was away from my station hospital detached to a general hospital. One night at about 10 p.m., I was standing with a flashlight at the side of a sleeping patient, counting his respirations. The O.D. had just been to see him and had assured me that he was not critically ill. In spite of what he told me, I really wasn't sure.

A wild-eyed nurse came up to me and told me she was my relief and that I should go and eat supper. I told her that I was probably going to skip supper because I wasn't happy with the way the guy looked. She looked at me like I had two heads and said, "That's dumb. Let me see his hand." With that, she reached for his nearest extremity. I was wondering to myself what she could possibly have accomplished by looking at his hand. Maybe she was going to see if his skin was dry and that he might be dehydrated, or maybe she was going to check his nailbeds to see if they were purple, indicating he might be cynotic, but I had already been counting his respirations.

I was absolutely floored when she opened up his fist, spread his palm and said to me, "He's going to be O.K.-- look at that long lifeline." I couldn't believe my ears, but after working at that nut farm hospital for a couple of weeks, nothing could have surprised me. I pushed her away from the bed and out the door yelling, "I'm definitely going to skip supper--Thank you!"

This was not a good thing to happen to someone who knew deep in her heart that she was the nearest thing to Florence Nightingale that God had ever created. I think this is the moment God chose to give Mickey her moment of truth. I think it's only fair to say that this nurse, who I didn't know from 'Typhoid Mary' was this institution's best practical joker. I heard later that everyone at night mess was hysterical when she related the story to the group. Everyone thought it was funny except me. When I threw her out because I thought she was nuts, she never came back to relieve me so that I could eat. She never did come back and I never did eat, so she proved I was right--she really was nuts.

I had been working on the surgical ward one night, while still on detached service, and was about to go off duty. This hospital had a Catholic chaplain and there was a Mass every night at 7 p.m. As I was rushing to get to the service, I stopped by a kid who called me for something. I noticed that his chest dressing was a real mess. I asked him when it had last been changed, and he told me that it never was, that usually a clean compress was just put on top of it. I realized the time for Mass was getting close so I told him that I really had to go, but promised him I would be back early the next morning to change the whole thing and clean it up. He said O.K. and I plopped a clean 4x4 on top of the mess and headed off for church.

I was kneeling down, trying to pray, but kept thinking about what a phony I was. I had left that dirty dressing on and was kneeling there playing the part of Holy Roller. I thought that perhaps God would be more pleased with me if I stopped the praying and did the dressing, cleaning up that bloody mess. I left the chapel and went back to the surgical ward, picking up enough antiseptic, alcohol, sterile dressings and tape to clean a squad-full of wounded chest.

As I removed each layer of putrid dressings, I felt more and more pleased with myself. When I finally reached his skin, I realized that I had probably been the first one to do a complete change on him since his surgery. I sincerely believed that I was the best nurse that had ever tended him.

I cleaned him up with alcohol, applied a beautiful sterile dressing and went back to my bunk, happy and proud with a new sense of holiness and spirituality.

I went on duty at 7 the next morning, going about my duties with a tight halo--it seemed that my head had enlarged during the night. I heard the ward surgeon, a Captain, scream out, "Who was the g.d. moron who touched this g.d. dressing?" He was pointing his finger at the chest of my new special patient. I ran over to him with the nurse, a 1st Lieutenant who was in charge of the ward.

Knowing that he was a little more than just displeased, I meekly replied "I did it, Sir." I wanted to die.

"Didn't you think," he asked me, "when you were cleaning him up that something different might have been going on?"

"No," I honestly answered.

"What did you think--if indeed you thought at all--what *did* you think?"

"Truly," I answered, "I thought everyone else was doing a half-assed job of it."

He was very quiet for a minute and then he burst into laughter. He told me later that he thought I was going to cry. When he laughed, the patient laughed, who said later he thought I was going to pee my pants. Then all the guys laughed. Before the laughter, though, they had all thought the doctor was going to punch me out.

Everyone was laughing except the 1st Lieutenant nurse who was in charge. She thought I had been referring to her as being half-assed. I myself didn't laugh. In fact, I could hardly breathe. My puffed up head had shrunk and I was being strangled by the halo that by then had slipped over my head and had landed around my throat, cutting off all air.

I guess I looked bad, because the Captain took me to the mess tent for a cup of coffee. In a very patient way, he explained the situation to me. He said that he and a doctor buddy had a theory that a healing wound would benefit more from 'skillful neglect'--that not messing with it and leaving it alone would be better than changing the dressing daily. The patient I messed with was his control and I had ruined it.

"How did it look," he asked. "Fine," I answered, and because he had such a sad look on his face I told him the story from my point of view. I didn't leave anything out, including the part about the angels I felt sitting on my shoulder while I had cleaned up his mess. I told him that I had had the best night's sleep since joining the Army--the undisturbed sleep of the Righteous Christian. He laughed and said I would have done well in the Crusades.

When I went back to the ward I asked the 'experiment' why he didn't tell me about what had been going on with the dressing test. He said he didn't have the heart to say anything because I had looked so happy while working on him. He said I hummed a song every time I pulled off a dirty compress. I told him he had no idea of how hard the mighty had fallen.

CHAPTER XXX

My leave papers arrived in the middle of April. Jim drove me to the Army airfield in Rome, kissed me goodbye and left me, supposedly to start my 30-day leave in the U.S.A.

The traveling orders read that the leave was to start when I reached Ft. Dix, NJ. The papers said Italy to Ft. Dix. They gave me the time. Securing the transportation would be entirely up to me.

I had been in Rome about 12 hours and had already been bumped from two flights. I slept on a bench in headquarters and ate at the Red Cross. A Captain told me that I would have a much better chance to get out if I would go to Casablanca and leave from there. I reminded him that my papers said Italy to Ft. Dix, not Africa to Ft. Dix. He insisted though, saying I would meet less 'brass' to bump me, and so I found my way to Casablanca.

On April 22 I got passage on a large transport. The pilot told me that it had been used by the 82nd Airborne. It had bucket seats against the side and the entire floor space was covered with stuff--engines and boxes--that were going back to the states. There must have been about 20 officers and enlisted men hitching a ride home. The pilot showed us how to blow up the Mae West vest we had to wear, how to inflate the life rafts we would have to use if we ditched and the steel helmets we could use if we got airsick. The fact that we had all this stuff to use worried me.

I had lost track of time so I don't know when we left. We flew for hours, bumping up and down in our metal bucket seats. A couple of guys were curled up in the aisle with their arms and legs wrapped around the cargo.

About three hours outside the Azores, the pilot came back to our area. He looked extremely uptight and said in a very husky voice that he had some bad news. I looked out the window and saw the Atlantic Ocean swirling below--way below--and thought 'what a way to end it.' I looked back at the pilot and he said they had just received word that our Commander-In-Chief, President Roosevelt, had died.

Everyone was very quiet as he went back to his cockpit. I felt this surge of guilt, because I actually felt relieved. Then a voice from across the aisle said, "Holy shit. I thought it was going to be us." We each then admitted that we all felt the same guilt. All of us were relieved that we had been spared doomsday. No one laughed.

We refueled at the Azores, were properly fed, and proceeded to an airfield where buses were waiting to take us to Ft. Dix. I was looking around for one I could take to New York or Brooklyn, when a civilian in a beat-up car drove up and asked me where I was going. When I told him my destination, he said to hop in. He was on his way home and offered to drop me off at a subway station in Brooklyn. We talked as he drove and he explained that the only reason he could not take me to my front door was the fact that he was low on gas and that it was rationed.

When I finally reached home, I was both happy and grateful to be reunited with my family again. My sailor brothers, Harry and Jack, were stationed in California so I didn't get to see them right away, but all the rest of the family were rounded up and we celebrated Irish-style. My mother embraced me and said, "Who is Jim Allen?" I had received three letters from him while I was travelling home.

The second day I was home, Pop asked me how long I could stay before returning to Italy. I told him that I would find out when I reported to Ft. Dix the next day. He almost died from shock when he figured out that I was A.W.O.L. According to Pop, that was not the way to do things.

The following day I reported to Ft. Dix, handed my orders to the Sergeant in charge, and held my breath. He peered at me, said I was two days late, and asked what had happened to me. I told him I had gotten lost in Brooklyn. He quickly looked at my home address and remarked how very fortunate I was to have gotten myself lost so close to home. He gave me new leave papers and said I was to return to Ft. Dix in 30 days. He also reminded me that it would not be too smart of me to fool around and to "be back on May 24." The war in Europe ended on May 14.

CHAPTER XXXI

It's impossible for me to describe my feelings when the war in Europe ended and I was stateside. I was happy about the war being over and being with my family again, but was sorry about not being with my gang to celebrate the victory. It was a very weird feeling. It felt like something had been stolen from me, like a prize I had won but was not going to receive or that my friends were giving a big party and didn't invite me. I was genuinely upset and was also ashamed to tell anyone how I felt. I tried to smile, but was really devastated.

I found that it was tougher for me to adjust to living here again than it was to get used to Africa. The war that I had just left seemed planets away. I went to night baseball games just like pre-war, a movie on Broadway just like pre-war and a dance with lights and music and partying just like pre-war. But things weren't the same. There were no signs of the war that had been such a big part of my life for what seemed like an eternity--no poverty, no hunger, no sad little children. It was hard for me to believe that the country was actively engaged in conflict.

It reminded me of something I had written home while in Italy: "…Thanksgiving Day I worked rather hard all day. At 7:00 when I got off I went to Mass. I heard a lot of ignorant and godless people say that they couldn't see anything to be thankful for 4,000 miles from home. Incidentally, do you realize the number of people who don't connect God with Thanksgiving Day? I am thankful almost every day that I am here. That is probably hard to understand because it is not worded properly. Let me put it this way: I may be walking along the streets in this devastated town and be wishing with all my heart that I were in Brooklyn until I see all the destruction and poverty.

Then I am glad I am in Italy and I thank God that He has spared the states this horror..."

One day after I arrived home, my mother sent me to the butcher shop with coupons to purchase meat for supper. I was amazed to hear all the women complaining and moaning about the small amount of food they could get for their rations. All I could think of were all the little kids at our camp, hanging around with their cans, collecting our leftovers to bring home to feed their families.

I could no longer contain myself. I told them how lucky they were to be so far away from all the death and destruction in Europe. I told them that there were hundreds of women in Italy, France and England who would have loved to change places with them. I stormed out of the store without any meat, and took a long walk. When I returned home, my mother told me that a neighbor had called and said she had seen me at the store. The woman asked if I had been sent home with battle fatigue. Her comment amused the whole family for weeks.

I read a book by Kurt Vonnegut, Jr., who described how the stateside view of the war affected him. In his story he wrote about the plight of a small boy who was stuck in an elevator between floors in a large department store. The boy wondered whether everyone in the store was upset and anxious about his safety and whether they were running around making plans to get him out safely. When the elevator finally started and reached his floor, the doors opened and he was amazed to see that everyone was walking around quietly, as usual. No one was upset and it seemed that no one even knew he had been scared and stuck in the elevator.

That is exactly how I felt. I didn't go through half of what Kurt Vonnegut, Jr. did in his war, but we both had exactly the same reaction to our return home. I missed being in action in Italy and I wanted desperately to go back.

Jim wrote every day, sometimes twice. He kept me informed about everything going on. He stayed in touch with the girls from my hospital (the 74th) and figured out how many points he had and how many he would need to get home. There were also a lot of rumors about who would be going to the Pacific Theater.

When my 30 days were up, I went to Ft. Dix to be reassigned. This time I didn't fool around. I wasn't in a playful mood. I was told that no one was going to Europe; the problem now was to get everyone home.

I was sent to Ft. Monmouth, NJ, the post I had departed from when I went overseas. I reported in to Major Newell, the same chief nurse who had been there when I left. She said she remembered me, but I don't think she did. She treated me much too kindly. For instance, if she had remembered me she probably would have brought up several things that had happened during my first time serving there.

One incident that comes to mind is when I was working the Eye, Ear, Nose & Throat ward. It was almost impossible to get the guys to gargle, so I would line them up in the latrine and have them gargle in harmony to whatever song was suggested for that day. We had quite a choral group going. She came in with the Colonel once and though I think he thought it was funny and a clever way to get the job done, she seemed to think it was quite unmilitary. In fact, there were several times I know she did not appreciate my fun way of doing things.

However, I ran into some minor difficulties and the good Major stuck by my side and got me out of any trouble. She notified me that I had been a 1st Lieutenant for two months. I was not impressed. The only thing that bothered me was that I could then be demoted but would still not be a civilian.

Jim Allen acted like I had personally signed the treaty to cease hostilities just so I wouldn't have to return to him. I didn't have the heart to tell him that Pop's cancer was only a skin cancer and very common to people of Irish heritage. But by the middle of May, Pop and Jim were exchanging letters weekly. All the family knew everything there was to know about Jim, and Pop was the one who told them.

I made my visit to Sister Mary Louise but spent so much time kneeling in the convent chapel that I had very little time left to speak with her. When we finally met, she told me that she knew I wasn't going to join them. I was surprised to hear her say it, but she reminded me that we had been corresponding for six years--three years of nurses' training and three years of war. She said the thing that concerned her the most was the way I fought all the Army rules and regulations.

"I don't think you had any more rules in the Army than I have had here in the convent. Yet look how angry you just became when I told you we had no more time to talk because you stayed in the chapel so long. You don't do well with rules."

I had to agree with that. I then told her about Jim and Father Farrell and the whole confession bit, and admitted that my meeting Jim wasn't by chance at all, but that I thought it was fate. She said that the nuns had been praying for me, but not to have me enter the convent. They prayed that I would remain spiritually safe and unchanged by the war.

It was a beautiful meeting with her. When I wrote and told Jim about the outcome, he wrote back immediately, declaring us engaged. He acted a little strange about it though. I didn't realize at the time that he believed if a man didn't present a diamond to his love, they would not be legally engaged.

Through the good graces of my father, Jim knew all the members of my family and so he sent money to my brother, Bun, to get me a ring. I believe I was the only girl in Brooklyn to receive a diamond engagement ring from her brother. Jim wanted a picture of me wearing the ring, but told Bun he didn't need to be in the picture. Bun said Jim was being a little ungrateful and that he could get his next girlfriend's ring himself!

CHAPTER XXXII

The final act of skullduggery I ever committed on an Army post was at Ft. Monmouth, NJ. The chief nurse had told me that because of time served on overseas duty I had enough 'points' for discharge from the Nurse Corps. I couldn't believe I was going to get an honorable discharge. I set off posthaste for the Q hut, where final physical exams were being done, before anyone could change their minds.

I caught up with Taffy, a fellow nurse who had just received the same news. She told me that if we rushed like all hell we could probably finish the exam, get back to barracks, pack and be in time to catch the 3:20 to New York City, a train which would take us out of the Nurse Corps and the Army forever.

We bucked the long line of guys waiting for their release by shoving and pushing and lying that we had to get inside to go on duty. When we got through the door we suddenly turned into patients. Taffy eyed a doctor she had been dating and said, "There's our man." He took our pulses, listened to our hearts, and asked if we hurt anywhere. When we said no, he handed each of us a little specimen jar and told us to give our last drop for the Army.

Wouldn't you know it. I couldn't go.

I thought of waterfalls, drank three glasses of H_2O, flushed the toilet, ran the faucet in the sink and did everything I had ever done to a patient to get their plumbing started. Nothing worked. Taffy started to get impatient and hung on the stall door, telling me to snap it up or we would miss the train. Completely defeated, I told her, "Taffy, I can't go. I can't squeeze a drop." She grabbed my bottle, poured half of her urine into it and filled each one to the top with water. I told her she was crazy, that whoever checked the samples would surely know that something was wrong, like, for example, the specific gravity.

When she stopped laughing (we both knew the odds that anyone would ever check it were slim) she said, "Let's take a chance. By the time they get to it, we'll be long gone."

So I put the urine bottle of top of the form I had filled out, '1st Lieutenant G.I. O'Reilly,' and in doing so got out of the Army the same way I got in--on someone else's pee.

CHAPTER XXXIII

It would be impossible to write my memoir without including the main character in the play of my life, Jim Allen. I always believed that our meeting was a gift from God.

I had received many blessings. The first one was to be born into my special family, who welcomed and accepted me into their midst. I never met anyone in my entire life with whom I would change places. Our home was always filled with unconditional love, affection and humor.

When I took and passed the entrance examination for the only girls' Catholic high school in Brooklyn, I counted it as a blessing that I really didn't merit. Before being admitted to the Norwegian Hospital School of Nursing I had to take a five-hour test administered by Belleview Hospital. I wrote that five-hour exam with a pen in my right hand and a rosary clutched in my left. When I was notified that the Norwegian Hospital Nursing School had accepted me, I considered it more of a miracle than a blessing.

When I was in high school, every time a test was scheduled I would have Pop wake me up an hour earlier so I could go to Mass before school. Every time Pop woke me up he would make the same speech. "If you spent half the time studying as you do praying, you would be a genius." I knew deep in my heart that I had a lot more faith than I did brains.

I was born August 12, 1919, and graduated from grade school in 1935. Thank God I was short and female. If I had been a boy, I probably would have been shaving!

The first time I had to repeat a grade was in the fourth. I had missed a lot of school because of a stubborn kidney infection. This infection was the reason I swapped a urine specimen with a complete stranger during my Army physical.

The second time I had to repeat a grade was in the sixth. The good nun, thin as a pencil and about six feet tall, was attempting to hang a swinging plant while standing on a moveable desk seat. The scholar sitting in front of me was supposed to be holding the seat still. I guess she forgot her duty. The seat went up, the nun went down. Her feet went up in the air and she landed on her rear with a complete lack of dignity.

Everyone laughed, but I, having had the best seat, probably laughed a little louder than the rest. Louder, but not longer. She picked herself up off the floor and glared at me. I tightened up every muscle in my body and prepared for what was coming. She screamed at me, "Do you think this is as funny, O'Reilly!" and hit me so hard on the side of my head that I was knocked out of my seat and onto the floor.

I took all the good blessings I could get. I prayed hard to get them, needed them and deserved them.

CHAPTER XXXIV

When the bomb was dropped at Hiroshima, I was happy that the war would soon be over. I was anxious for Jim to come home so we could be married and start a family. I had absolutely no guilt feelings about the horror of it or concern for the people of Japan who had been killed or maimed. Thank the Lord the war would soon end, I thought. I lived in this temporary state of euphoria for quite some time.

Both Jim and I were on terminal leave when we were married on November 10, 1945.

The Army got the last laugh on me, taking complete control of my life once again by snaring Jim into the Army reserves. Upon discharge, officers were told that anyone who didn't sign up for the active reserve would, if trouble developed with Russia (a strong possibility), be drafted back into the Army as a private. Jim said, "I was a private once and then I was an officer, and being an officer is much more preferable. Ha, Ha." I didn't laugh, but the subject was not open for debate. It was a done deal.

We got married and had nine children, eight girls and one boy. Every year, usually when I was pregnant, the old soldier would take himself off two weeks to play war games at Ft. Drumm. He said it was hard work, but I know he loved it. Every Thursday night, he took off for a reserve meeting and I know he loved that too. He spent endless nights at the dining room table taking courses from the War College. I know he loved *that*. He made Lieutenant Colonel and I know he really, really loved that.

After some time passed, I came to the realization that the atomic bomb was evil, but we couldn't discuss it. We always ended up in an argument.

In 1965 we took a cruise to Bermuda to celebrate our 20th Anniversary. We had a wonderful, relaxing time until one night when we were having drinks and conversation with another couple at the bar. The gentleman was another ex-warrior and the conversation was, naturally enough, about the relationship between Russia and the U.S. I wasn't enjoying the discussion and the hair on my arm was starting to stand up straight from the tension I was feeling.

When my Colonel husband, with his inflexible military mind, stated profoundly that we didn't have to take any crap from anyone because we had 'the big one,' I put my glass on the bar and slowly walked back to our stateroom. I was running cold water over my wrist to calm myself down when he came storming into our stateroom demanding to know why I had left the bar so abruptly. He informed me that I had embarrassed him.

"Embarrassed *you*?" I replied. "You would have been a damn sight more embarrassed if you had ended up sitting at the table with a cherry running down the side of your nose. I was that close to pouring my Tom Collins all over your head."

We knew we couldn't talk about the Army or politics. We disagreed completely on both. We had a happy marriage because we were usually smart enough to avoid those two subjects. With nine kids we had plenty of other topics of conversation.

I guess I caused him a few unhappy moments. I remember one night when we were all sitting at the dinner table, Jim at the head, me at the foot, with all nine children surrounding us. One of the kids asked me what the happiest time of my life was. Without hesitating or taking a minute to reflect, I said it was when I was in nurses' training--that it had been like my dream come true. The kids kept right on chomping away, but poor Dad suddenly turned pale. His eyes opened wide and he left the table. I followed him into the living room, knowing that I had upset him deeply. I asked him what was wrong.

"Do you realize," he stammered, "your answer was that the happiest days of your life took place at a time when none of us were involved in your life--at a time when you didn't even know any of us? Don't you think that's strange?"

I looked into the dining room and saw that all the kids were still laughing and eating. "It doesn't seem to bother the kids," I answered.

"Well, it bothers the hell out of me," he replied angrily.

I had to placate him with words of honey, but when I reminded him of the results of some stupid words he had expressed to his family years ago, he had to stop being angry. I think his boo boo was a lot worse than mine.

It happened when he took me to dinner to meet his aunt and cousins for the first time. We had climbed the stairs and were at the door when he grabbed my arm and said he had forgotten to tell me something. I got a strange feeling in my stomach and asked him what it was. Well, he answered timidly, he had three cousins who were in nurses' training and he told them they should never sign up for the Nurse Corps. He told them that Army nurses weren't among the most wholesome group and that they would probably regret it if they signed up.

With that, the door opened and he pushed me in. They greeted me warmly and acted nice and normal-like, but I wasn't going to let him off that easy. During dinner I said that they must have been surprised that Jim would bring a nurse home after what he had said about them. They laughed and said that they weren't going to bring the subject up and we all smiled. We all looked at Jim and waited while he hemmed and hawed and tried to come up with a weak explanation. It was fun watching him squirm.

We had a happy life. Lots of fun and love with all the kids. It was really tough on everyone when Jim became sick and was diagnosed with diabetes. He had to retire from the reserves after 30 years of service. The next year he developed cardiac problems and died in 1975 at home, surrounded by the family he loved so much.

One night years after Jim's death, I was discussing Hiroshima for the first time with my son-in-law, Tim.

He had been arrested because he had chained himself to the doors of the Federal Building on the anniversary of Hiroshima Day. During our discussion, he said how appalled he was that Americans had been so indifferent during that tragic time in our history. I told him that it was easy to be a Monday morning quarterback, but that when people are living in the moment, things aren't necessarily as distinct and clear. I was really angry with him and went to bed upset and unable to sleep.

I tried to figure out what made me so angry. I had never gotten angry before. We had stayed up many nights discussing the aggressive posture of the U.S. in most areas. I thought and thought, and finally was struck with the truth: On Hiroshima Day, on that day of infamy, I was so wrapped up in myself and in my life that I didn't care about the welfare of anyone else in the world. I had always been very critical of the German people in the treatment of the Jews. What we had done to the Japanese was just as bad or worse, and yet I never spoke out about it. I realized that I had never, ever said a prayer for the people who had been killed or injured. I resolved on the spot that I would take an active role in the peace movement and I did.

At that time I had three children living at home. The older six were married or away at school. I joined Pax Christi and became active in the peace movement, going to demonstrations but never risking arrest. I waited to do that until my youngest went off to college.

CHAPTER XXXV

There was a demonstration at Electric Boat in New London, CT. Electric Boat is where atomic submarines are manufactured. I was there to protest with a group of people from Pax Christi, a national peace group. A student from the divinity school group approached the leader of Pax Christi and told him that some members of the divinity class were going to be arrested on Good Friday. He asked whether our group would be interested in joining them. George told him that no one from our group was planning on being arrested, but that we would all be there to support them.

I went home and prayed and meditated. My youngest child, Roni, was living on campus at the University of Connecticut and I had no more responsibilities at home. I was about 65 years old and decided that if I was going to do any peace work, now was the time to get started.

Good Friday found me once again outside the gates of the Electric Boat Company. I had no idea of how to get myself arrested. I approached a young fellow named Chris, who I knew had been arrested many times, and asked him how I should proceed. He looked at me amazed and said, "Are you going to get arrested?"

I replied, "Yes--and I can't think of a better day than Good Friday to do it."

He told me how simple it would be. The first thing, he said, would be to go with the Yale kids, and when we got to the iron fence, to put my arm through the bars. He said that when the police order us to leave, I should say no. That would be it.

When the Yale kids were ready to go I went up to my friend, Maria, from the Pax Christi group and handed her the poster I was carrying. I told her to guard it with her life. It was a beautiful painting of a rose that my daughter Jackie had made and I treasured it. "Please take care of it," I begged her. "I'm going to get arrested."

I went up to the iron fence with the kids, put my arm through it and held on to the bar with all my might, waiting for the police to come. They started to drag kids away. A police Sergeant approached and read me my rights, advised me that I was standing on private property and asked me to move. I shook my head no. He repeated it. My heart was beating fast. My stomach was jumping up and down and I felt kind of faint. I shook my head no again and he placed his hand on my shoulder. He told me I was under arrest and asked me to walk to the police van. The minute he placed his hand on my shoulder, all the fear and anxiety left me. I almost felt Christ's arms holding me up. I knew I was doing the right thing.

The police took me to the waiting van and pushed me inside. All the kids were laughing and singing hymns and greeted me with, "Welcome, Grandma!" I felt great and joined them in song. The van started up but then stopped again. The back door opened and Joyce, another member of Pax Christi, was pushed in the door and landed on the floor next to me. I told her that I didn't think she was going to get arrested that day. She said she hadn't planned on it but knew it was going to be my first time and didn't want me to face it alone. They took us to the police station in New London and started to process us, taking our fingerprints, mug shots, etc.

Another van pulled up and emptied out. Chris entered with the crowd. I ran up to him and said, "I didn't know you were going to be arrested."

"Neither did I," he replied, "but when you said to me that Good Friday is a beautiful day to go to jail, I thought indeed it is, so here I am."

Another van pulled up and out came Marie, without my poster. As I approached her she said she had seen them put me in the wagon, then saw Judy lay down in front of the wagon and get thrown in. She thought to herself that if she believed everything I believe and everything Judy believes, then she should be in jail with us. She said the cops took the poster but "here I am."

We all left jail after signing a 'promise to appear' court document. It was the most beautiful Easter of my life, though not without complications.

My only son, Jim, had served on a submarine during the Vietnam War. Upon discharge he joined the Hartford Police and a year later, went to the State Police. He was horrified by my actions, and stayed angry a long time. Many members of the family agreed with him, as did friends. It was a rough period for awhile. I lost a lot of people who I thought were friends. Now they thought that I was crazy. My family stuck by me, although some let me know they didn't approve. I didn't preach or try to convert anyone. I took it as a personal thing that I just had to do. So I did it.

CHAPTER XXXVI

About a year after my initial arrest (followed by many more,) I overheard one peace worker tell the other that if anyone wanted to get arrested but did not want to do any jail time, then they should attach themselves to Mickey because she never gets thrown in the slammer.

I was a little upset, because that was true. The judges didn't know what to do with me. I reminded them of their mothers and grandmothers. One said to me once, "Why do I feel like I am sending my mother to jail?" I replied that he didn't have to send his mother to jail--we had been there since 9:00 that morning, so why not just give us time served. He did, and we all went home. The thing that bothered me was that I believe it isn't very brave to risk arrest if there isn't any risk involved.

The next time I was arrested, with about 50 other people, I refused to sign the 'promise to appear' document. They took me off to the woman's prison in Niantic, CT. It was one of the worst experiences of my life.

They put me in a holding cell with about ten young women who had been arrested for prostitution. They were all laughing because the police had taken the names and addresses of all the 'johns.' I guess they don't usually do that.

A matron took me upstairs for the admission 'delousing' shower, which was mandatory. She stripped off all my clothes and made me join the palms of my hands cup-like while she poured delousing solution into them. She had a watch and told me I had three minutes to shower. She told me to rub the lotion into my head, under my arms and in my pubic area.

People who are veterans at this, or even just a little bit smarter than I am, open their hands and let some or most of the soap fall on the floor. Not me. I was being the perfect prisoner and tried not to spill a drop. I poured it all over my head and did my armpits and pubic area with what was left. My head felt like it was on fire.

The matron led me--I couldn't see into the cell--and I met my cellmate, one of the young prostitutes. She was very curious about why I was in jail. I told her about the Italian village and the death of the baby girl, and that I considered the atomic bomb the work of the devil.

She was very quiet and then told me that she was a drug addict with two small children. Her parents had told her that if she didn't clean up her act immediately, they would begin legal action to take her kids away. She couldn't get help anywhere and had no money. Her plan was to raise hell during her jail time so that she would be pulled out and sent somewhere for rehabilitation. She said that she wasn't going to tell anyone but was telling me so that I wouldn't be frightened when she started her act. At about 9:00 she said, "Here I go," and started getting noisy. I told her I would pray for her, and then cowered in the corner of my bunk looking scared when they came to take her away.

My eyes kept swelling and were very painful. The nurse in the infirmary told me to wash them out with cold water. I lasted five days until my eyes closed and I couldn't see. I signed the 'promise to appear' document and called someone to come and take me home. There was no welcome home party for me. Some family and one old friend were angry with me for doing the action.

I visited the doctor I had worked for as an office nurse, and he gave me a lecture as he administered a cortisone shot. He was madder at me than the kids were.

But I had made a lot of friends in jail and felt perfectly safe there. The women called me 'Grandma' and became my protectors. I was arrested many more times, but I never did jail time again.

One time I was arrested and put into a holding cell all alone. A large group of male prisoners went marching by, staring at me as they passed. About 15 minutes later they returned, marching past me again.

One of the guys yelled, "Hey, were you arrested?"

"Yes," I answered.

He yelled back, "What for?"

"Soliciting," I shouted.

You never saw so many confused men. All I could hear was laughing and guys shouting, "What did she say, what did she say?" Needless to say, the police were glad to see me go.

CHAPTER XXXVII

The day after Clinton was elected President, he ordered the bombing of Iraq. This was unacceptable to me. My son-in-law Chris and I chained ourselves to the door of the Federal Building in Hartford and were immediately arrested, taken to jail, processed and given a date to appear in court. We appeared in court three times before our case was heard.

Chris is an eloquent speaker. He is very intelligent, and always has all the facts and figures at his fingertips. People listening to him always know that he really knows and believes what he is saying. He made a wonderful presentation. Since then he has traveled to Iraq eight times with a group called 'Voices in the Wilderness.'

I am exactly the opposite of Chris, and am scared to death to speak publicly. I don't know any technical terms or numbers. I can't remember names or dates. Worst of all, I get very emotional. Tears flow and my thought process collapses.

For instance, at one point I was trying to explain to the judge about how the bombing of the Italian village during the war affected me. Mothers who had already given husbands and sons to the conflict were now also forced to give up their small children and had suffered injury themselves. I tried to explain to the court the horror I felt while finding a villager who would tell a mother that her child was dead. I started to cry, and knew it would happen. I can't believe that 60 years after that tragic day, each time I recall the event it still saddens me so.

The only consolation I had in Italy was that I knew my country wasn't responsible for the destruction of that particular village. With the bombing of Iraq my country *is* responsible for the unnecessary killing of innocent women and children. I feel that I have to take a stand and declare "not in my name."

The charge against us was 'disturbing the peace.' At the end of the testimony, the judge said he felt that there were times when the peace ought to be disturbed. He then asked me what the penalty should be. I told him that we had been to court three times awaiting our hearing and on that day had sat through seven hours of appearances. I thought it would be appropriate for us to be given time served. The judge heartily agreed and we were excused from court.

In November, 2000, my daughter Jackie told me that she was going to Ft. Benning, GA, to join in a peace rally. The object of the rally was to protest at the "School of the Americas." This school takes in soldiers from Latin American countries to teach (or so the United States professes) tactics in leadership and government. We know, however, that these high-ranking revolutionary leaders have been instructed instead in more advantageous techniques of torture. The Salvadoran soldiers who were found guilty of the rape and murder of four Maryknoll nuns and the murder of a lay minister in 1981 were graduates of this school.

Other killings attributed to graduates of the School of the Americas are:

Assassination of Archbishop Oscar Romero (El Salvador)

Jesuit martyrs: The killing of six Jesuit priests and two women who worked in the rectory.

The El Mozole Massacre: 900 civilians killed in El Salvador

The U.S. Government has consistently denied that the School of the Americas was ever involved in any of this, but it is not surprising that the name of the school has been changed to 'Western Hemisphere Institute for Security Cooperation.' Don't get rid of it, boys. Let's just give it a new name.

That is what the protest was all about, and I wanted desperately to be involved. I talked Jackie into taking me with her. We flew to Georgia, signed in at a hotel and went to the rally at Ft. Benning. There were probably 5,000 protesters there from all walks of life--young, old, students, housewives, peace organizations, nuns, priests and ministers. I was wearing my "Veterans for Peace" sweatshirt and the organization itself was represented by many men with banners. The rally was a rousing success.

Martin Sheen was there. He climbed onto a stage that the organizers had thrown up and addressed the crowd. "As your acting President," (everyone laughed) "I give you permission to make your feelings known here today."

About 500 of us walked up the path leading to the entrance gate of Ft. Benning. We all crossed the over line drawn by the M.P.s. They told us that we were going to be arrested if we didn't stop. We all marched on undaunted. I think they arrested five or six people.

Everyone carried a white painted cross. Each cross bore the name of a person who had either been murdered or had 'disappeared' from a South or Central American country. As we walked, each of us kept repeating the name of the person on our cross in a prayer-like manner, respectfully and quietly. Many of us were crying as we walked and prayed. It felt so good to be there.

The M.P.s let us proceed for a mile or so and then stopped us. They loaded us into buses and drove us to a park about five miles from the Fort and dumped us out. I felt elated but was exhausted.

Jackie and I returned to the hotel, packed our stuff and headed to the airport for the trip back to Hartford.

Jackie left to check on our tickets and I sat where I could watch all the first class passengers board the planes. It was funnier to watch than a comic TV show. I decided that first class passengers are not only better dressed than tourist class, but they even walk differently. They seem to glide instead of drag. Of course, they also know they will have good food waiting for them--not like our plastic bag of peanuts.

I heard someone shout, "Where's Mickey Allen! I want to see Mickey Allen!"

As he approached, I could see it was Martin Sheen.

I answered, as loud as I could, "Mickey Allen wants to see *you*!"

I was out of my seat and into his arms in a flash. He gave me a big hug. He told me that he had just seen Jackie, who he already knew. During a 'Plowshares Action' she had thrown a vial of blood on a plane while banging on it with a hammer at Griffis Air Force base, and had done two years at a Federal prison. She is quite well known.

Martin told me that Jackie said I was 81 years old and had risked arrest. I told him that was true--me and about 5,000 other people, himself included. He said he was proud of me. We said "God Bless You" to each other, and I enjoyed my 15 minutes of fame.

I would work extra hard and die happy if Martin Sheen were elected the real President of the United States.

CHAPTER XXXVIII

We walked the Stations of the Cross last Good Friday, but things have changed drastically since the war with Iraq. The guards at the submarine base never did embrace us as friends, but now they act like we are terrorists. Now they are equipped with guns and they hold them at the ready.

I wish I could explain how I feel about these young sailors at the sub base. I look at them and see their grandfathers. But instead of eyes shining back at me with love, I see hate and mistrust. But I will always remember that fateful day in Italy.

That is the reason why I am at the Electric Boat Company in New London, CT, every time they are going to launch a Trident atomic submarine--The Ark of Destruction.

That is why I cross police lines and kneel and pray outside the gates of Electric Boat. That is the moment I think of when the cops are pulling me up off my knees and shoving me into a police van.

The Trident submarine carries 24 trident missiles, each with ten to 12 warheads, each warhead equal to 30 Hiroshimas. Seven thousand, two hundred Hiroshimas in one submarine, all aimed at women and children. It's my nightmare Italian city multiplied by millions. No. Not in my name.

I have been arrested, and will continue to get arrested for peace, because I believe I have a moral obligation to speak out against what I think is wrong. I believe that all the German people who stood by quietly when the Jews were being eliminated will have to answer to God for what they didn't do. I believe that I have a right to criticize my country when I think it is acting improperly. Yes, that chip on my shoulder is still part of me, and I wouldn't want it any other way.

I don't believe "My country right or wrong" or "Love it or leave it." I believe that some day I will face my Maker and will have to give an account of my stewardship. I want to be able to say, "I didn't accomplish anything, but I tried."

Who knows. God may just pat me on my head and tell me I misconstrued His words. But "Love one another" is simple enough for me to understand.

As of this writing we are still at war with Iraq, and I pray that the President will soon declare it finished. Our young boys are there now--probably grandsons of the kids I took care of in WWII. I would love to tell them that I'm not just some old lady working for peace, but a caring old Army nurse who just wants to stop war and bring them all back home.

As of today, I still wholeheartedly disagree with the Army and totally disagree with our Commander-In-Chief. I also would be scared to death if I were sent to the Far East. But as strange as it may seem, if I were 21 years old today, there's no question that I would serve my country as a member of the Army Nurse Corps.

LETTERS HOME

August 21, 1943

Dear Gang,

Just wrote to you day before yesterday, but here we go again. Things got quiet long enough around here to let a couple of us get away to a dance the Air Corps boys gave. You should see your little girl strut her stuff. These boys are so plentiful and girls so few that they aren't a bit fussy and consider any girl that can speak English a Ginger Rogers. We had passes until midnight but didn't get back until 1 so I guess all my fun is stopped for awhile while I get punished. We call our group of nurses' tents "Campfire Girls of America--Troop 74" and it drove the Colonel wild. We get treated worse than probies in nurses' training.

The other day Bob Hope and Francis Langford came out here to camp and put on a show for the boys. They were very good and everyone seemed to enjoy themselves. Poor Bob was limping around with a cane. He missed a foxhole the night before during an air raid. He'll probably talk about that when he gets back.

I met a friend of Jack's here yesterday who graduated from Our Lady of Angels with him. I wrote Jack about him. The kid sure acts nutty. I hope everyone at home is well and happy. I am writing this on Saturday because I don't dare write letters on Sunday. That's homesick day for me. It's not quite so bad now that we are kept busy, but I think of you all constantly. Please take care of yourselves for me, for if anything were to happen to you I wouldn't care if I ever got back. Write soon and often.

Love, XXXOOO, Sis

P.S. If this airmail gets to you any faster will you send me some air mail stamps? Otherwise, never mind. These were given to me by a patient.

September 1, 1943

Africa

Dear Gang,

Received a letter from Pop today. First mail in three days. I was very surprised to read that our V mail wasn't being filmed because yours to us is. Now for answers to your questions. The bathing suit did come but I wrote and thanked you for it. Secondly, you *can* send packages. All you have to do is show my request to the Postmaster and so help me I'm going to bust that fellow wide open when I get back if he doesn't let you. Thanks for trying, though, but please try again.

Today we had a little bit of cake for dessert. One to a customer. It tasted so good that I bought the gal's next to me for 10 francs (20 cents) so you see I'll soon go broke or die of malnutrition. Can you imagine a buddy doing a thing like that to a guy? The packages didn't come yet and I haunt the mail tent every night looking for them. I'll write as soon as they get here.

Mailman, I need – anklets, shoes, a sweater and a couple of head scarves and stockings. That takes care of him.

It is Wednesday 6:00 and I have just returned from supper and am now off duty. At 4:00 I got off, washed in my helmet (I am going to have it installed in the bathroom when I get home), donned my best slacks and went to my tent, collected all my Catholic boys who could walk and went to Mass. They were very happy because they said I looked so classy (a diaper wrapped around my head). I was the only nurse sitting with the boys. I told them that the only reason I sat with them was to make them behave, but they know that isn't so. They're really a swell bunch of kids and so grateful for any little thing I do for them. Tonight we are having movies out in the field and I have a date with 8 men ranging from the infantry to a parachute jumper.

Now Mom, I really don't need the sweater mentioned above, but you can fill in that space with edibles. No kidding, I am always starving.

These last two days have been terrible. We have had typical dust storms. The tents are covered with dirt and the latrine is filthy. What else? You know how much I miss you all and how much I wish I was home until I get on duty and talk with all my heroes. Funny thing happened today. This kid I have has been telling me all sorts of hair-raising experiences he has had up on the front. Today I caught him sneaking out of bed so I shoved him back and pulled down his mosquito netting and tied him in. Well, I happened to lock a bug in with him and you should have heard him yell. He screamed 'Mom' (that's 'me) so loud you could hear him a block away. He crouched up in the corner of the tent and yelled that the bug was advancing. You would think a bomb was headed his way. We all stood around him and laughed and the fellows told him to use some of the wonderful tactics he had been telling me about all week. I finally undid the netting and killed the bug and poor Joe hasn't opened his mouth all day. Here he is with a Purple Heart and is scared of an African bug.

Last night Oggie and I were frightened to death ourselves. We were walking to the latrine with our flashlights and didn't we walk plum into a kangaroo rat. We screamed and two guards came running, so I am not very brave either.

Have to end this masterpiece. I hope you have a wonderful time on your vacation but I guess by now it is over. Mom--

thanks for that beautiful holy card and Masses. I can certainly use them.

Good night darlings,

Sis

North Africa

September 6, 1943

Dear Mom and Dad,

Today would have been just another blue Sunday except when I stuck my head into the mail tent. Louie grinned and handed me 2 letters from Mom, 2 letters from Pop, a letter from Neil and a postcard from Neil III. So blue Sunday was turned into a happy one for me. I am so glad that you had such a wonderful time at Cape May. And you don't have to tell me how wonderful Jack and his grand bride were to you. I'll bet they are just as happy having you with them as you were to be there.

Your letters were all written while you were still there but I received one from Jack yesterday after you had left and he mentioned about Mom being lost in the evil caves. He said you would probably write to me about it, Pop. I am anxiously awaiting that letter to hear about how you got Mom into it in the first place, much less out of it. Your letters were so good and so very newsy. Mom--I guess you miss me almost as much as I do you. Pop--your really missed your profession. You should be writing books. The girls said to tell you that they love to hear your letters, as I can't help laughing at them. They always want to know the joke so I have to read the letters to them. Incidentally, thank you for the pictures of the W.A.C.S. Tomorrow I shall pin it up on my ward tent and make the boys salute it. I did that once before and when I came back into the tent after being out about ten minutes it was down and a picture of a fighting soldier was up in its place. They made me salute it.

I'll bet it almost kills you, Mom, to have to leave Jackie, Jr. down in Cape May. But you are home again with all the rest of the angels and you will be so busy that you won't have time to think of little stinky. I received a postcard from Romeo sent from Steeplechase and I tacked it up on my bedside table. Neil's letter tells me Butch is up and around on two legs and talks. He hasn't gotten to the pinching Mary Jane stage yet (His father hasn't told him yet that I want him to pinch Mary Jane until she writes me a letter). I'll bet Mary Jane thinks that I'm mean.

Marge and Betty went out swimming and should be back later.

Have to run now.

Love,

Sis

North Africa
Sept. 10, 1943

Dear Mom and Dad,

I wrote you a letter this morning but at mail call tonight darned if I didn't get another package from you two tonight and I just have to write again.

The pants and bra arrived today and they are perfect. Thank you so much for sending them.

Every time someone in our tent gets a package, Betty rips off the paper looking for candy. Margie got a package today and there wasn't any candy in it and Betty got mad. Bunny got a package the other day and no candy and Betty was as mad as all hell. Yesterday, when my package came and there wasn't any candy she made a big speech about us all writing home for clothes while she wrote and asked for candy. She said she hoped I'd never get another package as long as we are here. She also said she would never give us any more candy when she did get some.

Today at mail call we both received packages. I could tell from mine that it was all underwear and she laughed and laughed because she knew that hers was candy. She kept shaking her package and it rattled just like candy. She didn't stop shaking her box and reminding me that I wasn't getting any. Ha, ha -- she laughed. I opened my box, took out the clothing and she laughed even louder. As she was opening her package I was acting like I really didn't care what was in it, but when I saw her face I knew that something drastic had happened. So I ran to her cot to look. Do you know what was in the box? 48 WOODEN CLOTHESPINS. All told the four of us don't have eight pair of pants to hang up. Every day you wash your underwear and stick it up on top of the tent. It is completely dry in about five minutes. We couldn't stop laughing. I begged Bet to give me a clothespin so I could suck it like a lollipop. She read the enclosed letter from her sister who said that she read in the newspaper it was what the girls overseas needed. I'm still laughing.

Betty is funny and full of hell. Last week Margie ran out of socks and she asked Betty to sell her a pair of hers. Betty said OK, one buck. Bun and I got mad and called her a war profiteer but she insisted that since she had carried them all the way from the states they were worth the money. Margie wants the socks. I got the socks--one buck. I once paid her $3.00 for a bottle of perfume that probably cost her half a buck. The funny thing is that she would give you the shirt off her back if you really needed it.

There are three things keeping me from going crazy in this ratty, buggy, God-forsaken place--one is the fact that I am taking care of these wonderful guys. Two is our great chief nurse and thirdly the fact that I drew these three pick-of-the-crop gals as tentmates.

Bunny is a very serious person and very neat and orderly. Betty, Marg and I are loud and extremely messy. Because the tent is very small we only pass inspection because of Bun's picking and yelling at us.

Good night for now. I'll write to you again tomorrow so this will be a good letter week for you.

I love you,

Sis

October 23, 1943

Darlings,

Once again Lieutenant O'Reilly has assumed the role of night nurse. This time it is only going to be for two weeks. I have 14 tents, all surgical cases, and 8 corpsmen to help me, so it isn't really too bad. Oggie is on with me and we have just come from the O.R. where we had a cup of hot coffee one of the boys made, together with half a salami sandwich one of the doctors gave me and two hard boiled eggs a doctor gave me that some civilian had given to him. Did I tell you how wonderful the food has been lately? Really it's great. We have had fresh meat for the last four days. Everyone is mystified. What a relief from canned spam.

Tonight on my first rounds I went into one of the wards and found out that all of the patients were officers. They gave me some sort of phony line about my being beautiful. I really looked like hell. And then they told me they were hungry. I told them I was sorry but they would eat again at breakfast. They said again, "We are officers, and the last night nurse used to get us bread and coffee from her mess." Well, I almost blew my top. I am not too crazy about these gentlemen with bars and told them that their rank didn't rank with me.

I went into the next tent and told the corpsman there that the officers were not to have any food or coffee and have no privileges that the rest of the boys didn't have. Their lights were to go out on time and if he had any trouble, just to call me. One of the patients jumped out of bed and shook my hand and another poor fellow without a leg made me take a piece of his candy. They were so happy to see someone who stuck up for the enlisted men. That happened at 7:00. At 11:30 when I went to chow as I walked in I heard a fellow yell, "Here comes the champion of the dogfaces." It made me feel good. The nights lately are beautiful. Big moon. A million stars and a beautiful milky way to light up the skies. If you guys were here with me, it would be perfect.

A box of 8 delicious butter crunches arrived yesterday and they were <u>distributed</u> one to Bunny, Betty, Oggie, Marty, Captain Tall, Captain Share (Pappy), Lt. LoRe, and Captain Benito. And I'll be damned if I didn't forget to take a piece for myself. However, Betty also got some and she gave me one of hers. Thank you very much.

Good night, darlings.

Love,

Sis

November 5, 1943

3:30 am

Dear Mom and Dad,

Just your daughter in North Africa reporting that all is well. Two more nights of night duty will find me a Lieutenant with two days off and then a day nurse again. Remember how I used to sleep when I was home Mom? But not here. The only way I can sleep here during the day is if I take some sleeping pills and you know that is a hellish habit. The other day I fell into my cot exhausted and just got to sleep when a squad of enlisted men came with sledgehammers to fix the tent pegs and woke me up. The very next day I just hit the land of nod and the same mob came with shovels to dig rain ditches around the tent. The next day they came with hammers to put the wooden floor in. The next day we had to get up and get some of our uniforms. Soooo the next day I took 3 grains of nembutal and slept till about 6:30 p.m. When I woke up I had a regular jag on. I staggered up to the mess tent in the hopes of getting coffee to wake me up but didn't have any luck. I can't wait to get off night duty.

The only thing I am going to miss is to wake the guys up in the morning at 6:30. I go into the tents singing revile at the top of my lungs. Then 5 minutes later I go in and call them for school just like they were a bunch of kids and they react in just the right mood. They still call me 'Mom' and act like babies. This morning one fellow said that he wouldn't get up because he didn't do his homework. Another guy said I was being nasty because the old man had come in drunk and I was taking it out on the kids. Two others played sick and one guy jumped out of bed because he said it was his turn to go to the bakers for their breakfast rolls.

What a mob. You would never think they've been through all kinds of hell if you didn't see them all bandaged up for yourself. Rumor has it that we are going to be on the move again soon but don't know how true it is or where we are going.

Would you please do me a favor and give Mary Jane my clothes if they will fit her and my blue coat and red coat. Just keep the suits for me. And honey, I feel patriotic but I don't want any more war bonds. I will need all the money I can get after the war ends. Time to make rounds again. I dread leaving the tent.

Good night for now. Be good kids. Write to me soon.

Love

Sis

February 18, 1944

Dear Children,

This is my first anniversary as an Army nurse. I can't believe that all these strange exciting and happy things that have happened to me since the day I took my oath. All occurred during the space of one big year. I do know that I have doubly advanced in age and hope some in wisdom. I pray that next year this time will see me a happy civilian. Haven't heard from home in 9 days except for a letter from Bun 3 days ago. I hope all is well and that you are all safe and happy.

Mom--remember it was just a year ago that I took my leave of you? You'll never know how I felt leaving you sick like that in the hospital. Thank God that you pulled out of it safely. I realize that I owe quite a debt to God. It is a good thing that you people at home are praying for me. I am kept so busy praying for all of you back there that I can't seem to remember to include myself in them. I was terribly sorry to hear about Jack being sent to California. It must have made him very unhappy, especially leaving Kay and the baby. Will you send me his address just as soon as you get it so that I can write to him?

I received a letter from Doris Hanlon. She is in a station hospital in London and seems to like it fine. She wanted to be remembered to you folks and said to tell you that she hopes to be able to pay you a visit real soon. Incidentally, so do I. Aren't we an optimistic bunch? The sun has been shining brightly here these past three days, and you would be surprised at the changes it makes, both in the appearance of this mud hole and in everybody's disposition. Just as I finished that last sentence the wind started to blow and almost knocked down the tent. I guess you just can't predict anything about this weather.

We had company here in my tent last night. Every Thursday afternoon Father Lane comes and says Mass for us. At night he comes back and stays in our tent gabbing. Betty thinks he is a swell guy. He's the priest we met in town that first day we got here. I think I told you about his taking us to dinner.

Well, so long for now. Give my love to the gang.

Love,

Sis

Italy
June 2, 1944

Dear Mother, Dad & Gang,

Thursday night! I had been looking forward to this night for about a week because I had a date for a steak dinner followed by a G.I. Special Service Show. Today I came on duty at 7 a.m. and had a busy time of it. We admitted a very sick boy who needed a special nurse and the hospital provided one. At 3:30 I was all set to go off, take a shower and get ready for a luscious hunk of steak when in popped the chief nurse. Said she, "Lieutenant O'Reilly--I can't get a nurse to come on at 7."

"Does he really need a special?" I, in the usual manner, proceeded to blow my Irish top. She still insisted that she didn't know who to get, so here I am! I got off at 4, showered, drove hell bent for election in a jeep, had my steak dinner, took a rain check on the show and was back on duty at 7 p.m. So here I am. Guess I was just meant to be a night nurse.

I hope everything at home is OK. I haven't had a letter in almost ten days.

The weather here has been beautiful and the place looks like a massive garden. Poppies grow wild here--but like I told a fellow the other day--you're so wild about being here that you don't give a hootin' damn for the poppies anyway (I'm only kidding, Pop.)

Tonight they had a hymn singing over in the chapel tent and I could hear it here on the ward. Gosh did I get homesick. They sang all the old songs we used to sing around the piano at Norwegian Lutheran Hospital. I kept thinking of Hanlon and Nickie and Willie in England and wondered what they were doing; and Rita and Thora there in the states. I felt just like what I was--an old lady thousands of miles from home.

The way the war seems to be going now maybe I'll be home soon. Gosh--how I long to see you people again.

Our baseball team is coming along swell. I catch (mostly I miss) but it's a lot of fun and good for my tan.

Gee--it's so quiet here. Golden silence only broken by the occasional sound of crickets and airplanes. The airplanes give me a wonderful feeling of security (that is when they are ours) and an awful feeling of jitters when they belong to Herr Hitler.

The thrill of watching the symptoms and signs of a critical patient, with a searchlight, still prevails. Wow, what English--sounds like the critical patient has the searchlight but you know what I mean.

I guess I had better sign off. Good night, God bless you and write soon.

Love,

Sis

Italy
July 13, 1944

Dear Mother and Dad,

Here I go again and don't let me ever hear tell of you two complaining that I don't write often enough (That was meant for you, Mom).

Well, let's see – the weather is miserable—hot and sticky—the food these past three days has been foul tasting, poison and not enough to boot, mail has been very slow in coming from Brooklyn. The tents have quieted down some and I am picking up the weight that I lost. I guess that covers just about everything. Mom, will you send me Kay's new address please? I'll have to write to her seeing that she won't be getting your letters now.

We, a mob of the girls, were having a bull session in my tent the other night talking about Africa and Italy and home and all sorts of stuff. Someone asked what we would ask for if we could have anything in the world that we wanted. I wished that you could have heard some of the darn fool requests. I yelled out to hold a baby. I didn't even think. All I know is that my mouth waters every time I see one clean enough to hold without getting buggy. One wanted a room full of peppermint patties. Someone else a bath tub full of perfumed water. One even said an empty tub would do. She said she wouldn't mind filling it with her helmet (it's 16 months since we had a bath tub bath.)

When we were all finished we suddenly realized that no one had wished for the war to end or that we would go home. We all sat stunned until someone screamed, "Yee Gods--we're getting to like this kind of a life." Do you suppose that is so?

Yesterday they posted a notice on the bulletin board that two girls could sign up for a five-day leave at Sorrento. No one signed up and the chief nurse was delighted. I heard her remarking in the latrine that she was proud of her girls who didn't want to leave their jobs. I almost died laughing. We are all holding out for a crack at Rome and knew that a leave now would ruin our chances on that score. But needless to say, no one told the boss and she is still proud of us.

We had a big formal dance the 4th of July in our Officer's Club. You know evening gowns are forbidden because they are not considered part of our uniform. The Colonel decided that we could get away with it by calling it a costume party. I borrowed a honey of a pink one from one of the girls, silver slippers from another. One of the guys got me a beautiful corsage of gardenias from I don't know where, and what a time we had. It was the funniest sight I had ever seen – all the tents were messed up and full of clutter. I sat outside and had a very enjoyable time for about half an hour watching beautiful females in evening gowns, running from tent to tent. It was hard to believe that these were the same girls who such a short time ago were living in men's G.I. fatigues and washing in helmets. Maybe it won't be too hard for us to become civilized again after all, but to tell you the truth, society has me worried.

I have to stop now, take a shower and go to another lecture. This is worse than school ever was, only it isn't so bad to take when you look at the guy sitting next to you and realize that he has been a medical doctor or surgeon for about twenty years. Ha. Neither age, sex or education can get you out of these lectures.

Good night for now and God bless you always.

Love,

Sis

Italy

Sunday, July 17

Dear Mother and Dad,

Received your air mail letter dated July 6, Mom, and have a big fault to find with it. It's length. Gosh, but it was an awful little one. Do me a favor please and throw that stationery out of the window. All it is is a glorified V mail letter.

OK now. All is forgiven.

Last Wednesday night I got off duty at 3:30, showered, went to chow and then went with Oggie and a fun-loving gal by the name of Mary, to see our baseball team play a team from a nearby area on our field. The three of us (the only girls incidentally) sat on a little hill behind first base and heckled the visiting team to death. Really, we were unmerciful. The final score was 15 to 2 and as we walked back to the nurses' tent area we were in a very happy state of mind.

I don't know or remember, I should say, how normal, cultured happy girls act, but I do know that when an Army nurse is happy she can't keep her mouth shut, so as a result we walked home arm in arm, singing at the top of our lungs, "Old King Cole" (the G.I. version.) We got into the latrine and Mary said, "Wow--did you get a load of the Colonel?" Oggie said, "Yes, and now we're in a sweet mess." I always sing with my eyes closed. I didn't see the Colonel and asked them to explain the situation to me. Mary said, "He was standing by his hut (he has a carnival wagon out in the field painted and fixed up as cute as could be) giving us the eye and he didn't look too happy. I said that there would probably be a notice up on the bulletin board on the following day inviting Lieutenants Biehhold, Ogden & O'Reilly in to see the chief nurse and that doubtlessly we would all get hell. We washed up kind of quiet-like and walked outside.

Who stood there but the Colonel himself. We all saluted and started to creep away on our bellies when he asked us if we would come to his hut for a minute. We looked at each other knowingly with that "this is it" look in our eyes and said, "Yes, sir" and followed him across the field very meekly. We got inside the wagon very meekly and were quite surprised when he poured out four drinks, sat down facing us, cleared his throat and instead of giving us the expected tongue lashing said, "I'm a lonely old man--very lonesome and homesick at present and would really love to have you sing for me if you would be so kind."

Well, we almost died. That was at about 8:15. We didn't get back to our tents and we sang continuously until 1:00 a.m. Before we left he told us that hadn't had such a good time in 4 years. We sang all the songs we ever knew, including the 15-stanza Army Nurse Corps song we wrote ourselves (I made up about ten stanzas of it myself, which was wholeheartedly adopted by all the girls.)

Everyone was talking about us the next day. They said you could hear us all over the area. Now they call us the Andrew Sisters and we call ourselves Faith, Hope and Charity. He has stopped me about four times since then telling me how much he enjoyed the evening and he told the chief nurse that he never knew he had such talent in the organization. Truthfully speaking, we weren't good but we were loud and the songs were mostly cheer-up Army songs and it did a good job on him.

We are still pretty busy but sure would love to move out of here. Staying too long in one spot, even though it is a beautiful location, gets very monotonous. Bunny is still out taking her P.G. course in anesthesia and I miss her very much. Oggie is still a problem child, but her life is still hers and though I do plenty of worrying about her, I don't say anything.

Mail from home has been scarce, but maybe tomorrow will be a luckier day for me.

I'd give an awful lot to see Brooklyn right now. Gosh, but I get awfully homesick at times; almost all the time it seems lately.

Mom—about sending pictures to the girls: That one I sent to you that you liked so much is one that I had taken for our annual organization book and I only got it because the Sergeant in charge happens to be a very good friend of mine and made two up for me. I'll see what I can do about getting some other kinds though.

I guess I had better stop and get ready for chow. All I have had since last night's supper is a cup of coffee. It's too hot here to even bother eating.

Be good parents and write soon. And Mom please don't worry about me. Physically I am feeling fine and mentally I am almost cured. Time is the only thing to heal me up and I am stronger a lot more than I was two months ago.

Good night and God bless you both.

Your loving daughter,

Sis

Italy

August 5/6, 1944

Dear Mother, Father and Siblings,

Greetings, relatives. This writing every night is a bad habit, I'm thinking. If per chance I should skip a day Mom will be sure that I have been captured by the Germans or at least am at death's door.

Today I received mail from brothers Harry, Jack and Bunny. Aren't they darlings? Harry only wrote a page V mail and didn't mention his stinky Navy. I guess I really have him scared. I was getting rather sick of all his letters praising the Navy and razzing the poor old Army. Sooo when our 5th Army boys really started in moving, I started in heckling Harry, even with poetry. Since then he has written about the family, Aggie, the kids, the weather, but has always managed to avoid the war.

Brother Bunny gave me a report on the doings of my parents and I am happy to see you both managed to keep out of trouble. But brother Bernard does rub me the wrong way with his bitter essays on the doings of my Dodgers, as if I don't hear enough of that all night from these patients of mine. Pop, I don't like Bun's influence on Mom. Yesterday she said in her letter, "Bunny and Jean went to see the Dodgers get killed." Isn't that swell…and Mom living in Brooklyn all these years.

Brother Jack said, "Aggie and the kids arrived here last Friday and though only here about six hours, I saw them say they think California is a swell place--a snap judgement if I ever heard one." All of which shows that Jack is his same self, hating anything and place not spelled Brooklyn.

The ward is especially quiet tonight. What a difference from the first night I was on. Tonight when I put the lights out in the tents there were about four fellows who couldn't sleep so they sat around my desk and we were talking. They saw the letters from the boys and said that their sisters hardly ever wrote to them. I got to telling them about our J&S detective agency where Jack and I used to hide the boys' stuff and then find it for a fixed price, and how we made so much money until we tried it too often on Pop and he got mad and dissolved the corporation. And how Jack and I used to tear up the notes from school for one another (you never knew about that). And then I told them about Kay and Jack singing "For Me and My Gal" the night before I left the states and how after I got to Africa and heard it I cried. I got so damn homesick I sent the fellows to bed and they were all sorry they didn't pay more attention to their kid sisters when they were home. It made me realize how lucky I was and what swell brothers I had.

I told you about our dog, didn't I? Well, last night Oggie went over to the tent at about 1 a.m. to get her flashlight and I covered her tents while she was gone. She came running back panting and all excited and said, "Stupid (the dog) ate some rat poison!" You should have seen 'Mom' Markey. She took the dog in the nurses' latrine and gave it oil and stuck her finger down its throat. The kids said they had all they could do to keep her from calling the medical Officer of the Day. This morning when I got off duty I held the dog for her for about an hour. She seems to be O.K. now. She's the cutest thing, sleeps in your arms like a little baby and even wears a homemade nightgown.

It's a riot—the Colonel still doesn't know that we have her, but everyone else does. The doctors' tents are right next to the nurses but the Colonel has a little wagon fixed up out in the field so he isn't around. Someone said today that the doctors fed Vickie (short for Victory) the rat poison because she uses their area for a latrine, but it's only a rumor.

I am sending some more pictures, Mom. I had one of me on my cot but one of the patients took it and I don't know which of the 73 it was.

One picture here is of the outdoor movie I was telling you about. The other is of our nurses. We are 11 less now though.

Guess I had better stop before my conscience bothers me. I'll make rounds, then go to tent 8 and have coffee with Lt. Ogden. She's having a rugged night as she has a psycho boy who is very noisy.

Good night, darlings. Write and take care of yourselves.

Love,

Sis

Note: Censorship regulations originally prohibited me from stating in this letter that the leave I describe here took place in Naples

September 11, 1944

Italy

Dear Mother and Dad,

Hello again, darlings. Hope you are all OK. Mom, I received two packages today. One was full of cheese and tea balls and crackers, and one had the bathrobe, bra, stockings and candy. Everything was lovely. Thanks loads for it all. Mom, the nuts were good but just a little stale. Some of the girls get nuts from home in a mayonnaise jar and they stay fresh. And don't get me wrong now, I'm not griping. Betty, Marty, Leona, Kelly, Oggie and I were all having coffee at 11:30 a.m., our time off in our tent, when Mary brought over my package. It was almost fatal. The nuts were finished off in about five minutes. The crackers and cheese were also gone. We ate it up immediately. It sure tasted good. The cheese in the waxed paper was molded but we cut it off and ate it anyway. Thanks for being so thoughtful, darlings, we all enjoyed it so much.

I don't remember whether I was selfish when I was home but it is one good thing that I learned in the Army. Gosh it's just a natural established fact that what's yours belongs to the other guy. Food is never hidden. We put it out of the reach of the rats but everyone knows where it is at, and just helps themselves--not just your tent mates, but everyone. I hope we never forget how we rely on the other guy. This would be a miserable life over here if everyone was out for himself.

Oggie, Mary and I had an overnight pass to town last week. Let me tell you how I spent it. We got off duty at 3:30, dressed up in our Sunday best, piled into a jeep and rode into town. We reached there at ____. Can't tell you how long it took us (it's against censorship regulations). We signed into the hotel and were assigned to our rooms. Oggie and Mary had a beautiful double room with a balcony overlooking the harbor. But I want to tell you about my room. It had twin beds with a big soft mattress, a full-length mirror, a spacious closet (all we had were the clothes on our backs and a toothbrush) and I had a little bathroom all to myself.

We bounced on the beds for about half an hour and then decided to go to a show where "How Proudly We Hail" was playing. This show was forbidden to the troops because it was supposed to be bad for morale, so we knew that if we didn't get to see it now, we never would. We went downstairs and asked an Italian (the hotel, incidentally is run by the Army and our hospital has two rooms given to us by the General.) No other hospital has this privilege and only us because we are the farthest from town.

Anyway, this jerky Italian gave us directions and told us we could make it in 15 minutes but we knew better and gave ourselves an hour. Well we walked and walked and walked up and down side streets in total blackout through the slums. What a beautiful sightseeing tour it turned out to be. I thought I knew this town pretty well, but how wrong I was. The streets are very narrow and the 3 of us were holding arms and hanging on for dear life. For no apparent reason the sidewalks are cut into little sections, making a curb every ten feet. Oggie has pretty good night vision and every time we came to one she would yell 'step' and we would. We were passing a typical Italian homestead, one bedroom with about 15 people living in it right off the sidewalk open up like a Nedicks' shop. Naturally enough we all looked. No one yelled 'step' and bang! The three of us fell and reversed the tables and had all the Italies looking at us. We had on our nice, clean beige uniforms to make matters worse. Finally we found a boy on a bike and he led us there. It took us exactly an hour and ten minutes. We got there just in time for the last show. But I don't wonder that you got hysterical crying, Mom, when you saw it. We're not having it as tough as all that, believe me.

When we got out Oggie insisted that she wasn't going to walk back so she saw a nurse and Lieutenant sitting in a jeep and asked them to take us back to the hotel. We all piled into the jeep and when the Lieutenant tried to start it, nothing happened. He pulled up the engine cover and discovered that a very essential part was missing so off he went to get a replacement. The four of us stayed in the jeep until a big M.P. car pulled up. Out jumped a couple of Majors and cops came up to the car and started to check the number. They asked us where we got the jeep and I could just see the 3 of us in the stockade for the night. It seems that these fellows had also gone to the movie and had parked the jeep outside and as a precaution they had taken this roter (I think it is) out of the car.

The fellow who had our jeep had it locked so the stinkin' thieves, in order to steal the Major's car came to our car, which was locked, took this part, put it in the other car and rode away. The M.P.s fixed up our car. The officer came back and away we went. We got back to the hotel thirsty as the devil and went up to Oggie's room and stood on the balcony overlooking the harbor. It was really beautiful, Dad, and I was wishing that you were there to enjoy it with me. We decided that we wanted a drink and did it the easy way. I threw myself on the bed, grabbed the phone and yelled for room service. What a racket. We didn't feel a bit like Army nurses.

I went to my room, put my shoes outside the door, stripped and fell into bed. Oh yes--first I opened the window just as wide as I possibly could. And this window was about 3 times as big as my own in Brooklyn. I suppose I should tell you that I slept like a top, curled up in a real bed on a soft mattress. The truth of it is that I didn't sleep two hours. First of all I couldn't breathe. We sleep in tents that are open on 4 sides and have plenty of air conditioning. This room seemed so stuffy that I felt that I was being suffocated. Besides that, my cot is as hard as a rock and believe it or not I love it. It seemed to me that the darn mattress here curled up over my head and just gave away anywhere all at one time. At 8:00 my phone rang. The clerk reported that breakfast would be served until 8:30. I said thank you, hung up and turned over. I ached all over. I felt like a steamroller had gone over me.

Then the phone rang again. It was Oggie, who was next door and could have reached me by knocking on the wall. She said, "Mick, have you got all the men out of your room," and without even thinking I said, "Yes, they left early." She hung up fast and about ten seconds later in popped Mary yelling at the top of her lungs that these Italians didn't have a warped sense of humor like the Yanks and didn't we value our reputations. I never thought that the dumb Italian might be listening and when we finally went to breakfast we didn't dare look the desk clerk in the eye.

We had cereal, coffee, bacon and 2 (II) (two) fresh fried eggs, not dehydrated mind you, but just as the chicken lays them.

After breakfast we headed for Mass. Mary is Protestant but we grabbed her with us. We could have gone to any church. They have one on almost every corner. But we hiked to the main cathedral. It was really lovely but the Mass lost just a little bit of its dignity for us. You know none of these churches have benches like our churches do. They have regular little chairs and kneeling benches that can be moved. There was a little girl who came in late and didn't have a seat. We were all standing for the gospel at the time, so up she goes, takes a chair from behind a soldier and marches off with it. I thought we would all die. The poor soldier almost fell on his god-issued seat but saved himself just in time. Mary still insists that the Catholic churches are run mighty queerly. Poor Mary. Both Oggie and I had forgotten our wallets and she had to pay all our church money and they collected about 3 times.

After Mass we walked all over town and finally ended up at the Red Cross Officers Club. While we were sitting in the lounge we met a girl that we had known at Ft. Monmouth. She is stationed on a hospital ship and she told us that it was out in the harbor and that she knew for certain that two of our friends from Monmouth had no shore leave that day so we decided to pay them a visit.

September 15, 1944: Hey--had to stop for a couple of days. When we get busy I really work. Where was I. Oh yeah. We went back to the hotel for lunch (roast beef) and ate dinner with two nurses who were leaving for the states the following day. They had been over for 17 months and were as excited as two school kids at a birthday party. It gave me a funny feeling in the pit of my stomach to look at them and know that they would soon be home. It took a little bit of the kick and excitement out of our day's leave. We tried to tell them that we wouldn't go if we had the chance, but I don't think that we convinced them. In fact I don't think we convinced ourselves.

We started for the pier and as usual we got lost. It was drawing mighty close to 1:30, the time for the shore boat to leave for the ship. And when we finally got there they wouldn't let us past the gate despite our Lieutenant bars. So we had to dash, all dignity left behind us three blocks to the Port Authority office. We dashed back faster, if possible, with all kinds of cracks being thrown at us and when we finally got past the guard we didn't know where we were at. I saw two soldiers and asked them if they could direct us to the boat going out to the hospital ship and they had some sort of a convulsion, jumping up and down and started screaming down towards the end of the pier. Soldiers and sailors came out of nowhere and started yelling and whistling out to sea. When we got to the edge we saw what was causing the commotion. There was our boat 300 yards away leaving, heading for the hospital ship. After some frantic yelling they came and took us away. Then we proceeded to get seasick.

The girls (Oggie and I lived next door to them at Monmouth) saw us coming and what a reception we received. They showed us all over the boat, which held no patients at the time and treated us splendidly. What a setup they have. Two to a room with a little bathroom attached. We drank cold coca-cola until it came out of our ears. We talked about old times sitting out on deck and it seemed impossible to believe that these gals were fighting the war. Every time these ships hit the states the girls get a 15-day leave, so they had lots of dirt to tell us about the good old U.S.A. At about 4:00 they gave us bath towels, soap, powder, perfume and made us take a shower. Then they took us to chow. I won't describe the meal, but I am sending the menu. I had roast chicken (the real McCoy) and ate from china dishes, not tin. And knives that cut. Back at the hospital we get coffee once a day. Sometimes twice. Here they have it all the time.

What a life. But would I like it? No. Definitely no. Give me my tents and rough living any day. The girls treated us like we were infantry men from the front and when we left they piled us down with cigarettes, lighter fluid, soap, kleenex, toothpaste, peanuts, perfume and 8 cans of some chocolate drink. At 6:00 four of them came ashore with us and we spent a happy hour together. They left us to go to a dance and we piled into a command car from a nearby outfit. We reached our area at midnight, tired and loaded down with packages and very happy at having had a wonderful pass. We were exhausted though and how I greeted my nice cot.

Mom--I'm all dressed up in my new bathrobe. It is so cool and nice looking. Thank you so much. Guess I had better stop. I am going to send you some pictures we took of the three of us on that memorable day pass.

Love,

Sis

October 9, 1944

Dear Mom & Pop,

Tonight two of our pals from the 74th came to see us, bringing with them a box full of our candy ration, cans of fruit juice and some delicious peanuts, but we ignored all this and them because they also had some mail for us.

I received a letter from Doris Hanlon, who is in a station hospital in France, one from Mrs. McCoy and one from you, Dad. It was written on August 16 and mailed on September 16. I think you made a mistake in the month. It was a beautiful description of the storm. You did just as good a job as any picture possibly could. It is wonderful to think that you and Mom are so healthy but please don't go around tempting fate. I guess you know how important you both are for my morale. I don't blame you for being proud of yourselves but please promise me that you won't go around exposing yourself to all the elements.

You know when we first got here the place was just lousy with flies and bees so we told the enlisted man who brought us to bring our mosquito nets and canteens with him next time he came in. The girls were telling us tonight that the Colonel himself brought the stuff into us. They said he was so funny when he was telling the story back at the hospital. He said that he walked into this beautiful building loaded down with blankets, mosquito nets and canteens and said that he looked very out of place. He said he was as mad as all hell because they had us living in tents in all this splendor. He said he walked up to some Major and asked to see the commanding officer. They said they were sorry but the commanding officer was not in. "Well," says the

Colonel, "'who's next in charge?" so the led him to the adjutant's office. The Colonel said he marched in full of dignity and in a very brisk-like manner plopped all the junk on the adjutant's desk and in a mighty tone said, "I brought this stuff for my girls in the tents." He said he was mighty disappointed because the fellow didn't say anything and therefore the poor Colonel couldn't argue.

He's a honey. He's for us about 100 % and it is a great feeling to know that your C.O. is behind you, come what may. We still hate it here. Oggie is awful. She shows her dislike so plainly. We all walk around with a 'chip on our shoulders.' These gals are only overseas a year so naturally enough we consider them all as rookies and don't take any fooling around. We didn't get our whiskey ration from them and griped plenty about that although I still have all of last month's left yet.

I was so happy to hear that Jack got a leave. Be sure to tell me how he looked and acted. Oggie's cousin came to see her right before we left and he couldn't get over the change in her. I wonder what your reaction to me will be. I know that I have changed an awful lot, not too much for the better, I'm afraid. I have a very independent air about me and will tell anyone to go to hell at the slightest provocation, but I guess civilization will straighten me out plenty.

Pop, if you value your health, you had better stop sending me all those W.A.C. pictures. About two weeks ago when I received that letter with all the pictures enclosed, the whole mob was in my tent having coffee. The next day at lunch Mary handed me an envelope and said, "Read this." I opened the envelope and out fell six pictures of W.A.C.s. I let out a yell, reached across the table, smacked her and spent the rest of the day dodging the chief nurse and Colonel. So please don't start any trouble.

Once again, darlings, I must say good night. Sweet dreams, be good. Take care of yourselves.

Love,

Sis

October 10, 1944

Dear Mom & Pop,

I guess you know that I am away from the 74th at a general hospital on detached service. I hate it pretty much but I have gotten used to a little bitter with the sweet so we are just working along and praying that we will soon be called home to our good old tents and mud.

This setup is really beautiful--All modern buildings, marble floors, running water and all modern conveniences. But we don't like it at all. It's funny when you live in a certain tent and associate with the same people you get to call it home even though you feel like running away from it many a time.

Although all the regular nurses live in a beautiful building, we nurses on detached were put into a tent. It isn't fixed up as cozy as ours at the 74th because we took a long time to fix ours up with ration boxes and clothes racks and sheets (that we took from the hospital). Besides, at home we are only four in a small tent, whereas here, we are ten in a big tent. Six of the girls are from another station hospital, one girl is from Brazil and the three of us. The girls that live with us are all 'swell people.' Naturally enough we all get along great because coming from a station hospital, we can all sympathize with each other and gripe about the way these general hospital people run things.

A general hospital can be compared to a station hospital as Kings County to the Norwegian Hospital. They are much larger and have a census about 4 times more than ours. They have a lot more help than we have and therefore don't have the same family atmosphere.

Tomorrow afternoon Oggie and I are off and have the entire following day so we are both going to go home overnight. We phoned up the hospital and they are sending us the necessary transportation.

Sis

October 10, 1944

Things here at this General Hospital are exactly the same. We still hate it. It's funny--Oggie, Leona and I have been living robustly in tents for 18 months and suddenly one week here working in a building, we have all developed colds. Tonight our 74th dietician (she was in the last war and mothers us to death) came to a meeting and dropped in to see us in our tents. She was horrified to see:

1. Leona massaging her feet because they were all swollen from the marble floors (we were used to mud or dirt.)

2. Oggie draining her sinuses, and

3. Mickey nursing a honey of a cold.

She said she was going to hurry home to the boss to tell her to get us the hell out of here.

If it weren't for the patients I think I would go over the hill. They are a swell mob. All casualties, and all in wonderful humor. I doubt if my disposition would be half as good if I only had one arm or leg.

Love,

Sis

Italy

October 44

Dear Mom and Pop:

Before I get too far let me tell you the circumstances I am fighting while I am trying to write:

1. Leona is reading a book while scratching her head. That in itself doesn't sound too bad, but it is a nasty habit we are all trying to break her of. So consequently I have to keep one eye on her and one eye on the paper.

2. Oggie received 14 newspapers from home and insists on reading out loud to us every five seconds. I was just informed of the price of beef--how many ration coupons for canned ham and all the country news. She's terrific, mispronouncing everything.

3. They finally put a stove in our tent. It is not coal and we are afraid that it will explode any minute. We are all gathered around it like a bunch of hicks in a country general store. And Sylvia, a nurse from Brazil, has her can in my elbow. Otherwise this is a beautiful time and place to write a letter.

Nothing new has happened except that we go to bed exhausted every night at 8:00. Really, I don't think I ever worked as hard in all my life but what work. It is really wonderful and no one gripes about it. Last week Oggie and I went back to the 74th, stayed overnight and returned here the next day. What a wonderful reception we received at home. Major Mack took us up to his clinic, packed our sinuses with argyrol, sent us for ultra-violet light treatment and fed us because we both had such bad colds. We were mad at him because we really wanted to get pneumonia so that we could stay there and not come back to this *&% hellhole.

Oggie is reading again. Somebody just received a letter from a fellow in England consisting of 40,568 words. Comments Oggie after reading the clippings:

1. What dope counted the words.
2. Pity the poor Lieutenant who censored it.

I don't mind Oggie reading the news, but her remarks at the end of each paragraph slay me. Oggie was kind of annoying reading out loud to us but it really enlightened me on the cost of living back home. It must be terrible. I think it's a sin when I think of how we all leave food on our plates over here. So don't send any more food, honey. We get coffee from the kitchen and steal bread from the mess and always eat at night. I am getting as fat as a house....

EXCERPTS OF LETTERS:

New Years Day, 1944

...We had a turkey dinner at 6:00 and at 7:00 I took myself to Mass and Communion. It certainly seems funny to eat a big meal an hour before receiving Communion but that is the way we fighting people do it. We have no fast because we are in a combat area and are not supposed to know what time the next meal is coming. What a laugh that is. If you are more than 10 minutes late they won't feed you. We also eat meat—spam--on Fridays...

...Our Novena services are coming along very successfully. The crowd gets bigger and bigger instead of thinning out as we thought it might. I have a new name now--Sister O'Reilly. The boys want to know when I am taking my vows. I really have a lot of fun gathering them together for church services at night. Last night, for example, I got off at 4:30 and washed up. When I went back to the ward at 7:00 they all started to moan and scream with pain and protested vigorously when I went around pulling them out of bed. But they really want to go. They stop right in the middle of a card game or a book and if they are sleeping, demand that I wake them up...

At a different location...We don't have any Mass on Sunday. We nurses are allowed to ride over to ____ in an ambulance but no patients can come. The priest comes out here on Thursday instead. But we do have Protestant services. Last Sunday church call sounded and I went around rounding up all the Protestant boys. They used to laugh at the Catholics tripping out on Thursday. One fellow asked me if I knew which side I was on. But they felt mighty happy to think I would get them out as anxiously as I would the Catholics. We have 40 beds to a ward and I didn't have any trouble with any of them.

One fellow said he wouldn't go because his feet hurt him. I got kind of disgusted and walked away from his bed with the remark that more than His feet hurt Jesus when He was on the cross. When I looked out the tent a little later I saw him hobbling off to chapel so I guess his feet stopped hurting him.

I have talked to all these fellows and they all tell me the same thing. They say they haven't done much praying since they were little kids but when they are up there on the line with shells going off over their heads and bursting near them that they really pray as never before.

Yesterday an officer called me over to his bed and showed me a miraculous medal novena booklet that he carried with him all the time. He said that every day without fail he said the prayers and made the novena. He said, "Mickey, I'm not a kid and I'm not a holy holy, but I really believe in my heart that the only thing that has kept me alive are the prayers of my wife and family and my own faith in God." He was a big, burly guy and he was so sincere when he said that that even if I didn't believe in God myself, he would have set me thinking…

January 1, 1945:

Happy New Year! Home alive by '45--that was the motto on the walls this morning and for some mysterious reason everyone seemed to believe it. I certainly hope that it is true. One fellow came running up to my desk snitching on Lawrence because when they were singing "Home alive by

45" Lawrence started screaming, "Golden Gate in 48." Naturally enough, I had to take disciplinary action. Lawrence made a formal apology and sang the '45 song to us until we all got so tired of it we sent him out scouting for rumors...

...I guess I forgot to tell you that Peter died. I think he froze to death. I put cotton in a cup and covered him with more cotton. Then I wrapped a big wool coat around the cup to keep him warm. When I got up in the morning to feed him, he was just like an icicle. Just as cold and as hard. Betty said I suffocated him and what I felt was rigormortis. But I don't think so. Anyway, I have no more baby...

...It is early in the morning and I am a little tired. I have 60 officer patients under my care. Tonight a fellow called me outside and presented me with a beautiful thick, juicy steak sandwich. It seems that this afternoon a Naval officer was admitted and he didn't like our good old Army chow, so he got in touch with his Captain who immediately came to his rescue with typical Navy food--steak. What a tough life my two kid brothers must be leading. Ho. Ho. I hope that gets to Harry. I can smell them burning now.

Good night, darlings, be good children until I get home. Mom, do you remember that you always used to write that on the notes that you left for Jack and I if you went out while we were at school? Good night again.

With all my love, Sis

...We are getting up in the world. We were invited to have some cocktails with a General so the three of us had a very lovely time. We didn't relax very much as we are mere 2nd Lieutenants and have to watch our steps a little bit. If you remember, Mickey, Mary and Oggie make up that famed trio that loved to sing so much. My heart was in my mouth all night for fear the highball would loosen me up and we would start serenading the General, but everything turned out OK. The Colonel I was with was a former congressman from North Carolina, very witty and as clever as a stinker. We had a good time.

When we get home about 11:30 we ran into the latrine giggling like a couple of schoolgirls. Who was there but the chief nurse. First we had to convince her that we were sober because she did not believe we spent the night being entertained by the General. After we had convinced her she turned to Oggie and said, "Did Lieutenant O'Reilly offer to help the General out of any difficulties he might be in?" Then I got mad and went to my tent peeved. Did I ever tell you about the incident she was referring to? It happened in Mateur, North Africa about a month after we had set up, only a different General…

Note: When they were discharged from the hospital, many patients wrote thank you notes which were always a pleasure to receive, but this was a very sad one. When John was under my care he told me to write to his brother in the states to get paper so that I could get copies of pictures made. This was the reply I received:

1943

Dear Mickey O'Reilly,

The day after I received your letter, I received a telegram notifying me that John was dead. He thought a lot of you nurses, and especially you. I want to say "thanks again" for helping to make his short time in Italy and on this earth happy. I don't imagine it will be long before I'll be in Italy also (if I have my way.) If so, perhaps I will be able to convey my gratitude in person.

I sent a few packages of printing paper, but not knowing what contrast you wanted, I sent some No. 3. If you will just drop me a line telling me how many dozens, or gross, and what contrast, I'll be glad to send them. I will also try to 'corral' some 620 film. I believe that is the size you use (?) Please send the information as soon as you can, as I'd hate to receive an answer somewhere in Italy. But kidding aside, it's no trouble and I'd like to do it, as this is one of the few requests Johnny ever made of me.

It seems strange, when we were young, we would fight constantly, and then as the years roll by, you gradually draw closer and closer together. This last year, being in the same company, I found that we were as close to each other as any brothers could be. That's one of the reasons why I find it so hard to reconcile myself to the fact that I shall no longer see him.

Sorry, guess I'm sorta' carrying on--

Sincerely,

Ted Akimoto

Editor Note: The following letter is included over the objection of Mickey Allen.

Letter Published In "The Tablet"
(Brooklyn Paper for the Catholic Dioceses)

"Former Patient Praises Army Nurse O'Reilly"

Dear Sir:

It was quite a surprise to me to look at the front page of The Tablet and find a picture of Lt. Genevieve O'Reilly, of the Army Nurse Corps, facing me. It's been quite a long time since I last saw Lt. O'Reilly and so your article and the many excerpts from her letters especially interested me.

I was fortunate enough to be one of Lt. O'Reilly's patients in North Africa for a few weeks during October, 1943. The hospital itself did not have much to offer in the way of atmosphere until we patients got to know "G.I." O'Reilly-- and then it became known as "Casa O'Reilly." (Our favorite nickname for Lt. O'Reilly was "G.I.," and it was something of a contradiction, of course. "G.I." signifies living strictly according to the letter of the Army regulations; Lt. O'Reilly, however, had her own way of handling some of the "red tape.") The hospital at which I met Lt. O'Reilly was a Station Hospital, located a few miles outside of Mateur, in Northern Tunisia. The countryside was bleak and almost completely barren. We were just coming into the rainy season, which meant a frequent flood through the wards of our "tent city." Furthermore, our rations at that time were on the meager side: "bully beef, dehydrated cabbage, etc." over and over again. In spite of these drawbacks, "Casa O'Reilly" was the nearest thing to home which we had seen in the Mediterranean Theatre of Operations--all because of Lt. O'Reilly.

Of "G.I'.s" nursing abilities little need be said; she hovered over her patients constantly and tirelessly like a mother-hen over a brood of chickens. I am certain that the medical authorities find her a really good "right arm" in the restoration to normal health of their patients. However, it seems to me that it was on the psychological side that Lt. O'Reilly did her best job. Her personal interest in each patient, her keen sense of humor and her cheery disposition were just the tonic which each one of us needed. A bit of the "Tomboy" personality was a big asset, too. I can still hear her "Come on, you guys, it's time for church," or to one of her more active patients, "Put up your dukes" as she squared off in a John L. Sullivan pose. Her entire attitude toward her work is best summarized in one of her own letters, as printed by you: "I think that contentment is three quarters of the treatment which these boys need." All of this should not be taken to mean that a patient could do as he pleased while under "G.I.'s" supervision. I recall a few instances where Lt. O'Reilly's Irish temper was let loose on one of the boys, but here she was always justified. As a matter of fact, when this did occur, all of the other patients were on her side in the matter, and when enlisted men side with an officer against one of their own kind, that is news!

Mr. O'Reilly says that he regrets that "the mother's wives, sweethearts and sisters of our wounded boys do not know of the devotion and loving solicitude of our Army nurses." Our Army nurses are undoubtedly doing an outstanding job, especially those of them who are serving overseas. However, Lt. O'Reilly is one apart; there may be thousands of wonderful nurses caring for the men in uniform, but there is only one "G.I." O'Reilly.

Joseph V. Novotny, Jackson Hts.
    (Discharged from U. S. Army Air Corps at Ashford General Hospital, White Sulphur Springs, W. Va.)

PHOTO GALLERY

Jim and I on our honeymoon

Somewhere in Africa

The Infamous "Latrine"

*The ocean makes us far apart
But there's a spot deep in my heart
That no one else can ever own
That heart's for you, dear Mom alone.*